Stairway to the Upper Room

Stairway to the Upper Room

Daily meditation on the
Gospel Readings for Sundays
and Solemnities

Volume II

Ronald Walls

GRACEWING

First published in 2003

Gracewing
2 Southern Avenue, Leominster
Herefordshire HR6 0QF

ISBN 0 85244 570 9

Typeset by Action Publishing Technology Ltd,
Gloucester GL1 5SR

Printed by MPG Books Ltd
Bodmin PL31 1EG

CONTENTS

PREFACE

Not for the first time, the indefatigable Fr Ronald Walls
has done us all a service.

There is no shortage, happily, of commentaries on the
Mass readings provided by the Lectionary. But this
volume, as its catching title indicates, has its own distinctive approach. It stands out in two ways. First of all, here
are no dry as dust exegetical notes on the inspired texts,
nor, on the other hand, mere pious ramblings which
have little to do with what the Bible is actually saying.
Rather, Fr Walls' reflections on the readings deftly insert
the passages of a particular Sunday or Solemnity into the
full sweep, the whole course, of biblical revelation as
understood, transmitted and celebrated by the Church in
her eucharistic liturgy. This is in accord with the big-
hearted, truly 'catholic' approach to Scripture urged by
Vatican II's *Dei Verbum*, and answers the cry of so many
listening hearts. Secondly, these volumes provide a guide
to meditation and prayer. In this, they reconnect with the
ancient link, cherished by the Fathers of the Church and
monks, between reading (*lectio*) and prayer (*oratio*). Thus
prayer, our poor word to God, is rooted where it should
be rooted, in God's word to us, and can take on a new
truthfulness. And it is rooted, not in our own sometimes
too subjective picking and choosing, but in the Church's
calm, liturgical breaking of the bread of the Word,
Sunday after Sunday. Once again, Fr Walls has refused

to separate what belongs as a whole, and so helps us towards a richer, more integrated Christian life.

May this work lead us up the stairway of Scripture into the presence of the Lord!

Dom Hugh Gilbert, O.S.B.
Abbot of Pluscarden

INTRODUCTION

This book contains two volumes. The first is devoted to the Scripture readings in the Sunday liturgy which present Salvation History, the tale of the wonderful deeds of God, through which the salvation of mankind has been accomplished. That tale is told partly in the readings from Advent to the conclusion of the Christmas season on the feast of the Baptism of our Lord, and partly in the readings from Lent to the end of the Easter season at Pentecost, to which the feast of the Blessed Trinity and the feast of Corpus Christi are appended. Between the Christmas season and Lent there is a variable number of Sundays in Ordinary Time, and so Volume I includes Sundays 2–12 cycles A, B, and C in Ordinary Time.

Volume II is devoted to the readings for the Sundays 13–34 in Ordinary Time for all three years. The 'ordinary' weeks of the liturgical year are the time when the Christian's attention is directed to the task of perfecting discipleship, of growing in sanctity. Volumes I and II of this book together provide a guide to daily meditation for every week in the three years of the liturgical cycle. Before beginning to follow out the programme of meditation suggested by this book, it may be helpful to consider for a moment what is distinctive about Christian prayer, in particular about Christian meditation.

Prayer

The moment we set foot upon the first step of the stairway of prayer, the urge is born in us to climb up until we find rest in the Upper Room of God's presence. We share the feelings of the psalmist who sang: 'As a doe longs for running streams, so longs my soul for you, my God' (Psalm 42.1). And we are encouraged by the grace of God to believe that this desire will in the end be satisfied. 'What we are to be in the future has not yet been revealed; ... when it is revealed we shall be like him because we shall see him as he really is' (1 John 3.2).

But the Christian who longs for this consummation must be patient; the mere longing to see the face of God does not all at once and without more ado introduce the worshipper into the immediate presence of God. If the initial 'cry of recognition and of love', as St Thérèse of Lisieux called it, is to lead on to union with God, the cry of recognition and love must come to terms with the recognition that we have fallen out with God. St Peter became painfully aware of this when our Lord enabled him to haul in a great catch of fish in the Sea of Galilee. Falling down at Jesus' feet he cried out: 'Leave me, Lord; I am a sinful man' (Luke 5.11).

Men and women cannot by their own moral strength reinstate themselves as friends of God and climb back into paradise. Their only hope is that God comes down to them. This hope has been fulfilled. In the Person of his eternal Son, God has come down to earth and reconciled us to himself; and so, at the heart of the Christian Faith stands the affirmation: 'The Word was made flesh, he lived among us, and we saw his glory, the glory that is his as the only Son of the Father, full of grace and truth. From his fulness we have, all of us, received' (John 1.14, 16).

On the eve of the Reformation in Scotland, the poet William Dunbar applauded this act of divine condescension in an *Ode On The Nativity*.

Sinners be glad and penance do,
And thank your Maker heartfully;
For he that ye might not come to,
To you is comen full humbly,
Your soules with his blood to buy,
And loose you from the fiend's arrest,
And only of his own mercy;
Pro nobis puer natus est.

The incarnation of the Son of God is the foundation upon which mankind's redemption rests, and is the reality that makes prayer possible. In prayer we want to turn our minds to God, but how do we do this, upon what do we fix our imagination? In St John's Gospel we read: 'No one has ever seen God; it is the only Son, who is nearest the Father's heart, who has made him known' (John 1.18). And so we fix our imaginations and our minds upon the sacred humanity of our Lord, Jesus Christ.

Christian meditation
Meditation for the Christian is that form of prayer which consists mainly in concentrating attention upon the Person of Jesus Christ, upon his actions and his words, for just as it was through his flesh and blood that he redeemed us, transforming us into his own kith and kin, so it is through his sacred humanity that he teaches us and leads us on through prayer towards perfect union with God the Father. To express this thought St Catherine of Siena used a simple and vivid metaphor. God speaks to her:

My sublimity stooped to the earth of your humanity and together they made a bridge and remade the road. And why? So that you might indeed come to the joy of the angels. But it would be no use my Son's having become your bridge to life if you do not use it. (*Dialogue* XXII).

St Teresa of Avila teaches exactly the same truth, stressing that our Lord's sacred humanity is the only means by which we can reach the heights of contemplation. This is what she wrote to Fr Garcia de Toledo:

> It is God's will if we are to please him and he is to grant us great favours, that this should be done through his most sacred humanity, in whom, his Majesty said, he is well pleased. I have seen clearly that this is the door that we must enter if we wish his sovereign Majesty to show us great secrets. Therefore, Sir, even if you reach the summit of contemplation your reverence must seek no other way: that way alone is safe. (*Life* XXII).

Catherine and Teresa were two great Christian mystics, women who through prayer found a very high degree of union with God, and their method was to apply their minds and imaginations to the Person of the incarnate Son of God. Their type of mysticism and of prayer stands in sharp contrast to all other forms of mysticism and the methods of meditation associated with them.

For the nature mystic, union with the deity is achieved by a natural progress, because the substance of the human spirit is regarded as of a piece with the divine Spirit; in its union with God the human soul simply realizes all its natural potential. The beatific vision, on this view, consists in reaching a certain psychic state, progress towards which can be advanced by natural means, such as ascetical practices, hypnotic chanting, even by the use of hallucinatory drugs. For the Christian mystic, on the other hand, God always transcends human nature, and although the end of mankind's redemption is union with God, that union, on the Christian view, is not a merging of like substances but a loving union between persons who remain distinct. The meditation through which the Christian hopes to come ever nearer to union with God makes no attempt to alter the psychic state of the worshipper. All effort in Christian meditation is devoted to coming to know the Christ portrayed in the Gospels, and to listening to him.

It is true that the Christian should pray constantly, for prayer, as St John of Damascus said in the eighth century, is the 'raising of the mind and heart to God'; but there are times when it is appropriate, and indeed necessary for spiritual progress, to set aside times for meditation, times when one makes a conscious effort to get to know our Lord and his teaching better. These are times when it is wise to follow our Lord's advice: 'When you pray, go to your private room and, when you have shut the door, pray to your Father who is in that secret place ...' (Matthew 6.6). The words with which in the eleventh century St Anselm of Canterbury opened his classic work, *Proslogion*, remind us that there is an important place in the Christian's life for the prayer that requires temporary withdrawal from the hurly-burly of life:

> Come now, insignificant man, leave behind for a time your preoccupations; seclude yourself for a while from your disquieting thoughts. Turn aside now from heavy cares and disregard your wearisome tasks. Attend for a while to God and rest for a time in him.

This book is designed to help us meditate systematically and with perseverance upon the Lord who is presented to us in the Scriptures. We will discover, however, that meditation, important as it is, is not the end, but a step in progress towards the consummation of prayer, a consummation that comes not through our effort but from God's gift.

The structure of this book
Because the subject of meditation is the Person and teaching of our Lord Jesus Christ, the most important item for each day's meditation is therefore the Gospel passage, which is indicated but not printed out. In every case it is the Gospel reading for a Sunday or Solemnity, and

appended to this is a short Gospel commentary. This is not an exhaustive exposition of the reading, but merely a stimulus to the intellect and imagination, for meditation ought to be one's own work. Provided also is a short text from the Old Testament which throws light on the main theme of the meditation. This too is often taken from the Sunday liturgical reading, as is the vocal prayer in the form of an excerpt from a psalm. Daily meditation during the week is treated as a continuation of the worship that took place on Sunday.

A method for meditation
Meditation is not the activity of disembodied spirits but of men and women who are flesh and blood, and so like all human activity is learned and can be improved by good technique. At first, learning a technique, going through a sequence of moves, may seem somewhat artificial, but it enables a person to act habitually with ease and efficiency. Each one must pray the prayer that he can pray, but as a rule meditation progresses through a series of phases.

1. Having resolved to meditate daily, one should decide prudently when and for how long one will meditate. Most busy people find that fifteen minutes is a sensible length of time to spend in daily meditation. At what time of day this can best be done depends upon particular circumstances. Having made a decision, however, one should abide by it. People sometimes experience emptiness of mind and dryness of spirit after completing a period of meditation, and become discouraged. Although we may think that nothing has happened during our meditation the Lord will reward in some manner our sacrifice of time. We say that time is money: no one likes to waste time, and so making a sacrifice of a little time-span to be offered to God alone is in itself a declaration that no one is more important than God; it is an act of faith, which is what the Lord desires most of all to find in us. At the end of a day when we may have felt that our meditative prayer never got off the ground, we may well discover that the

whole day has been blessed with amazing tranquillity and a sense of accomplishment.
2. Read the Gospel passage carefully. This may be done at leisure on Sunday at the beginning of the week or on the evening before the meditation is to be made. It is useful to have the Gospel passage at hand whilst one is meditating, so that memory can be refreshed if need be.
3. Make a brief examination of conscience. This is essential because prayer cannot be severed from life, and nothing so much impedes prayer as a disorderly life. This *examen* is better done on the evening before the meditation, and it should not be prolonged. It is counter-productive to become too introspective during meditation. St Teresa of Avila gives wise counsel on this subject.

There is no state of prayer, however sublime, in which it is not necessary to go back to the beginning. And self-knowledge with regard to sin is the bread which must be eaten with food of every kind, however dainty it may be, on this road.

Then she warns against the temptation to wallow in self-analysis.

But bread must be taken in moderate proportions. It will be wiser to go on to other matters which the Lord sets before us, and we are not doing right if we neglect such things, for his Majesty knows better than we what kind of food is good for us. (*Life* XIII).

4. Immediately before beginning the meditation proper, two preliminary petitions ought to be made. The first is for the gift of total detachment from every worldly interest or care; the second is for grace to understand whatever is presented in the Gospel text, so that it may transfigure our lives. These petitions may be expressed in one's own words. Here are two models:

a. Almighty Father, give me grace to desire only to serve and praise your divine Majesty; free my mind from every concern, and lead my thoughts to your incarnate Son, so that I may return to you, our Father in heaven, and in you find peace.

b. By the light of your Holy Spirit, Lord, enable me to understand what I have read in the Gospel, and to be transfigured in accord with what I have learned. I ask this through Jesus Christ our Lord.

5. When the curtain rises as a play begins, we focus our eyes on the set and on the characters who are about to live out the drama. So it is with Scripture-based meditation. In imagination we see the physical setting in which characters begin to act and to speak.

Ignatius of Loyola recommends that meditation can best begin by our attending carefully to the details of the physical setting. This will anchor our mind and imagination. Following this we should listen carefully to the words of our Lord, and also to what the other characters say. Likewise we take note of all that is done by the characters and all that happens to them.

6. Next we try to understand our Lord's teaching and the meaning of the action. This part of the meditation may prompt us to study the Faith more diligently, but such activity cannot adequately be carried out in fifteen minutes' meditation, and in any case we ought not to prolong this phase of meditation indefinitely, for there is more to meditation than seeking to understand.

7. From this phase of meditation, wherein the imagination and intellect are active, we move more deeply into the Gospel scene, seeking now to stand on the stage with our Lord, to be in his presence and to speak quite naturally with him, as one speaks to a friend.

St Teresa of Avila describes how, long before she became a nun, she used to meditate:

My method of prayer was this. As I could not reason

with my mind, I would try to make pictures of Christ inwardly; and I used to think I felt better when I dwelt on those parts of his life when he was most often alone. It seemed to me that his being alone and afflicted, like a person in need, made it possible for me to approach him. I had many simple thoughts of this kind. I was particularly attached to the prayer in the Garden, where I would go to keep him company. I would think of the sweat and of the affliction he endured there. I wished I could have wiped that grievous sweat from his face, but I remember that I never dared to resolve to do so, for the gravity of my sins stood in the way. I used to remain with him there for as long as my thoughts permitted it. (*Life* IX).

If we persevere in this sort of meditation, after a time we shall become aware that we are rising higher and higher up the stairway of prayer until finally we arrive at the door of the Upper Room.

Contemplation

Behind that door is the Holy of Holies, the sanctuary of God's presence, and once in that room we have entered the contemplative phase of prayer; but we cannot force entrance, we must knock and wait until the Lord opens the door for us, and walks with us into the room, just as he walked with the Twelve into the Upper Room to institute the Holy Eucharist. In that room through the sacrament of his Body and Blood he enabled them to enjoy, as never before, communion with God the Father.

We must bear in mind that our Lord's purpose was to open up for us the way to the Father – 'No one can come to the Father except through me' (John 14.6); but when he has opened the door of the Holy of Holies for us he steps aside. At the Last Supper he affirmed: 'When that day comes you will ask in my name; and I do not say that I shall pray to the Father for you, because the Father himself loves you for loving me and believing that I came from God' (John 16.26–7).

Having accompanied us up the stairway and ushered us into the Father's presence, our Lord's work is complete; his function as Mediator between the Father and mankind has been accomplished; he no longer stands between us and the Father but beside us, leading us in adoration of his Father who is also our Father. Members of his Body, living by his Spirit, sharing in the life of the Blessed Trinity, we are caught up in contemplation of the divine Majesty. In this ultimate phase of prayer, imagery and intellectual activity are left behind; relaxed and in silence, our minds and wills become aligned with the mind and will of God the Father, who blesses us with peace and the assurance of seeing him as he really is in the kingdom of heaven.

At the end of our times of active meditation we leave space for this element of passive contemplation; then we round off our meditation with

Our Father . . . .

The Meditations

SUNDAYS IN ORDINARY TIME, CYCLE A

Sunday 13(A)

Old Testament thought:
The woman: 'Whenever he comes he can rest here.'
Elisha: 'Next year you will hold a son in your arms.'

(From 2 Kings 4)

Vocal prayer:
   I will sing for ever of your love, O Lord,
through all ages my mouth will proclaim your truth.
Of this I am sure, that your love lasts for ever,
that your truth is firmly established as the heavens.
Happy the people who acclaim such a king,
who walk, O Lord, in the light of your face.
who find their joy every day in your name.
   I will sing for ever of your love, O Lord.

(From Psalm 89)

Gospel: Matthew 10.37–42

In the Christian moral order filial and family duties rank very high. Concluding his instructions to the Twelve, Jesus emphasized the urgency of their work by affirming that devotion to preaching the gospel must take precedence over even such duties. No apostle has a right to neglect normal duties to parents or children, but if such duties come in the way of the work of spreading the gospel, they must take second place.

This precept implies complete detachment from all earthly affections. Taking up the Cross means relinquishing all claim to earthly comfort and ease. An implication of that is that the apostle – in the sense of the ordained servant of the Church – cannot apply his mind to material affairs; and so our Lord continued his discourse by pointing out the responsibility of other disciples to assist in the work of the apostolate. Addressing the Twelve he said: 'Anyone who welcomes you welcomes me.' He had in mind those who provide for the necessities of those whose work is the preaching of the gospel and the care of the Church. There are examples in the Gospels of people who served Jesus himself in this way.

The Old Testament prophet Elisha on his travels enjoyed the hospitality of a Shunemite woman. An important feature of the story is that she was rewarded with a son – new life. Her New Testament counterparts will be rewarded with eternal life.

Sunday 14(A)

Old Testament thought:
Rejoice heart and soul, daughter of Zion!
Shout with gladness, daughter of Jerusalem!
(Zechariah 9.9)

Vocal prayer:
I will give you glory, O God, my king,
I will bless your name for ever.
I will bless you day after day
and praise your name for ever.
The Lord is gracious and full of compassion,
slow to anger, abounding in love.
How good is the Lord to all,
compassionate to all his creatures.
The Lord is faithful in all his words
and loving in all his deeds.
The Lord supports all who fall
and raises all who are bound down.

(From Psalm 145)

Gospel: Matthew 11.25–30

Jesus had been rejected by the religious leaders. His words recorded in today's Gospel are his response to that rejection. The truth he preached and the mystery of who he is remained hidden to these, 'the learned and the clever'. These men were learned in all the details of the Law; they knew by heart all 613 precepts; and some of them prided themselves on keeping them. But this very expertise blinded them to the essential Law and to its origins in the loving Wisdom of God.

The 'mere children' were the poor souls in Israel, who did not even know what these rules were, and who, in any case, would have found it impossible to observe them. Jesus described these people as those 'who labour and are overburdened'. To these people – all of us – Jesus promised relief from these pointless, artificial burdens, replacing them with his own 'yoke', that is with the genuine Law of God. But before asking us to take it up he explained how it becomes possible to carry it with ease.

The key to spiritual tranquillity through keeping the Law is to know the Father as he knew him; and such knowledge of the Father comes only through knowing Jesus.

By the gift of the Spirit which he has given us we are able to share his filial relationship with the Father; and so our ability to keep God's Law is born of our seeking to know him through Jesus. This knowledge enlivens in us a sense of obligation, but even more it awakens in us an awareness of God's loving design for each of us. His yoke fits perfectly so that we become able to pull the particular load that each of us is given.

Jesus says to each of us: 'Come to me . . .' Christian life centres in turning to Jesus and acknowledging him as the only way to the Father.

Sunday 15(A)

Old Testament thought:
The word that goes forth from my mouth
does not return to me empty.   (Isaiah 55.11)

Vocal prayer:
You care for the earth, give it water,
you fill it with riches.
Your river in heaven brims over
to provide its grain.
And thus you provide for the earth
you drench its furrows,
you level it, soften it with showers,
you bless its growth,
you crown the year with your goodness.
Abundance flows in your steps,
in the pastures of the wilderness it flows.

(From Psalm 65)

Gospel: Matthew 13.1–23

The thirteenth chapter of St Matthew's Gospel contains seven parables of the Kingdom of God. The Kingdom of God is the rule of God amongst men and women. That rule is manifest in the life of the Church, and so the parables are descriptive of the Church.

The first parable is about Jesus's use of parables. 'Why', asked the disciples, 'do you speak to the crowd only in parables?' Why could he not have put things to them in a straightforward way? Was he deliberately making it difficult for ordinary people to understand his teaching?

In replying, Jesus did not deny that it is difficult for people to grasp God's word, but the difficulty is not of God's making, it is of mankind's. Jesus said: 'They look without seeing and listen without hearing', and then he quoted Isaiah: 'Their ears are dull of hearing, and they have shut their eyes, for fear they should see with their eyes, hear with their ears, and be converted.' It is not God's desire that they should fail to see and hear; it is men and women who fear that they will hear and understand and be converted. Here lies the problem: men and women do not want to be converted and align themselves whole-heartedly with God's will. The human race is plagued by an in-built resistance to the will of God, and this makes them deaf to his word. A parable reveals and yet hides the truth. Men and women have to make an effort to discover its meaning. This effort is the sign that they genuinely wish to live in harmony with God's will. If they possess a humble and attentive disposition, they will begin to understand the parables and Jesus's teaching in general.

Sunday 16(A)

Old Testament thought:
From the top of the cedar I will take a shoot
and plant it myself on a very high mountain.
It will sprout branches and bear fruit.
Every kind of bird will live beneath it.

(Ezekiel 17.23)

Vocal prayer:
O Lord, you are good and forgiving,
full of love to all who call.
Give heed, O Lord, to my prayer
and attend to the sound of my voice.
All the nations shall come to adore you
and glorify your name, O Lord:
for you are great and do marvellous deeds,
you who alone are God.
But you, God of mercy and compassion,
slow to anger, O Lord,
abounding in love and truth,
turn and take pity on me.

(From Psalm 86)

Gospel: Matthew 13.24–43

The parable of the Sower is followed by six parables of the kingdom. These may be described as parables of the Church, because the Church is the society in which God's rule over mankind is focused.

The first parable is about the Church in the world. It is the place where God rules, but all members of the Church are not equally submissive to his will, for some are children of the Evil One. These individuals are difficult to distinguish at first from God's children, just as the poisonous weed, zizania, in its early stages of growth, is very difficult to distinguish from sprouting wheat. When the workers offer to tear out the weed, the farmer warns them that as the roots of the weed and wheat are now intertwined, too much damage could be caused to the wheat crop. This parable does not depict a sharp division between the Church and the world, but sees the world as potentially the mystical body of Christ, which will be manifested in glory only after the Day of Judgement. While this world lasts the face of the Church will suffer disfigurement.

The second parable of the kingdom sets aside the question of the relationship between the Church and the world, portraying the Church as a great tree, rising up from a very small seed to provide a home for the birds of the air. The Church is a safe house for all men and women.

The third parable returns to the topic of the Church in relation to mankind at large. The world is a lump of dough, the Church the leaven which transforms it into a nourishing loaf. The stress here is upon the efficacy of the leaven, the mysterious power of the ecclesial, sacramental reality of the visible, identifiable Body of Christ on earth to sanctify men and women in every generation.

Sunday 17(A)

Old Testament thought:
And so I prayed, and understanding was given me;
I entreated, and the spirit of Wisdom came to me.
Compared with her, I held riches as nothing.

(Wisdom 7.7–8)

Vocal prayer:
My part, I have resolved, O Lord,
is to obey your word.
The law from your mouth means more to me
than silver and gold.
Your will is wonderful indeed;
therefore I obey it.
The unfolding of your word gives light
and teaches the simple.

(From Psalm 119)

Gospel: Matthew 13.44–52

Today's Gospel reading concludes the reading of seven parables contained in chapter thirteen of St Matthew's Gospel. The final parable returns to the theme of the parable of the wheat and the poisonous weeds. It tells of the severity of judgement that will be passed upon the wicked at the end of time. 'When it (the net) is full' is a significant phrase, indicating that sorting out of the fish cannot be done while the missionary operation of the Church is still in progress.

The other two parables form a pair. They present the kingdom of God as the kingdom or rule of God within each member of Christ's body. In Old Testament literature, treasure and pearls symbolize wisdom. The Church has attached the reading about Solomon's prayer for wisdom to the Gospel for today in order to alert us to the meaning of these two parables. Nothing can be compared in value to wisdom, divine wisdom, which is utterly different from human cleverness. The true believer will be prepared to pay any price in order to possess this wisdom.

Sanctity comes to us mainly through the direction of our lives by wisdom. Wisdom is the mind of God himself; and in so far as we come to know God and live according to his mind, we are sanctified and qualify for entry into the end-kingdom of God, when the net is finally landed, when the field is totally harvested.

Sunday 18(A)

Old Testament thought:
Listen, listen to me,
and you will have good things to eat
and rich food to enjoy.   (Isaiah 55.2)

Vocal prayer:
The eyes of all creatures look to you
and you give them their food in due time.
You open wide your hand,
grant the desires of all who live.
The Lord is just in all his ways
and loving in all his deeds.
He is close to all who call him,
who call on him from their hearts.   (From Psalm 145)

Gospel: Matthew 14.13–21

Matthew records three occasions on which Jesus withdrew to a safer place: when he was taken as a child into Egypt; when he moved out of Judaea into Galilee on hearing of John the Baptist's arrest; and in today's Gospel when he moved away to a lonely place on hearing of John the Baptist's execution. Jesus knew that the hour when he would offer himself in sacrifice for all of mankind had not yet come and so until that hour arrived he took evasive action when he was threatened. In today's Gospel reading the loneliness of Jesus is stressed – a hint that only he could make atonement for humanity's sin.

The people had by now become so impressed by his words and presence that they were prepared to go out in search of him, forgetful of the need to take food with them. When the crowd found Jesus he made no attempt to hide from them, but showed compassion on them by healing their sick and then providing food. By this act Jesus proclaimed his creative power, his divinity. He also, by his command 'you give them something to eat', foreshadowed the authority of the apostles to nourish the Church in time to come.

For the Jew, bread signified the word of God; and so by this miracle Jesus affirmed that he is the final word of God, both in respect of his teaching and also in his very presence. The miracle possesses also a eucharistic significance, telling us that the bread of the Eucharist will provide real food for mankind for all time. Jesus's gesture of raising his eyes to heaven, described in this scene, was carried over by the early Church into the action of the celebrant when reciting the Canon of the Mass, although the gesture is not mentioned in the record of the Last Supper.

Sunday 19(A)

Old Testament thought:
Alone I encircled the vault of the sky,
and I walked on the bottom of the deeps.
Over the waves of the sea and over the whole earth,
and over every people and nation I have held sway.
(Ecclesiasticus 24.5–6)

Vocal prayer:
The Lord is king, with majesty enrobed;
the Lord has robed himself with might,
he has girded himself with power.
The waters have lifted up, O Lord,
the waters have lifted up their voice,
the waters have lifted up their thunder.
Greater than the roar of mighty waters,
more glorious than the surgings of the sea,
the Lord is glorious on high.   (From Psalm 93)

Gospel: Matthew 14.22–33

Matthew 13.53–18.35 portrays the Church as the first-fruits of the kingdom of heaven. The Church was to endure for all time, not just while our Lord was on earth, and so the teaching and miracles of our Lord, recorded in this section of St Matthew's Gospel, possess a symbolic and prophetic character, telling us about the nature of the Church in the time after Jesus had ascended into heaven.

The miracle of the loaves and fishes had foreshadowed the Eucharist. Today our Lord's ascension is foreshadowed by Jesus going up alone into a mountain, symbol of God's dwelling-place, while the disciples are left on their own and sail off in a boat – a symbol of the Church throughout the ages.

A storm blows up; the disciples battle with the waves and become afraid. This incident may be an allusion to their desolation after his death, but may also be seen as a symbol of the recurring experience of the Church down the ages.

Jesus now returns, walking across the water towards them. They are terrified and think he is a ghost. This detail hints at his resurrection appearance, when they thought they saw a ghost, but were reassured that it was truly himself.

From now on Peter is given a prominent place in St Matthew's Gospel. Peter is the first to show signs of faith and trust in the Lord; he even dares to imitate our Lord by stepping out onto the water; then, at first so confident, he hesitates; fear returns and he begins to sink. Peter typifies the human spirit wavering between faith and unbelief. 'Lord, I believe; help my unbelief.' When we pray in this humble manner, the Lord always helps us get back into the boat.

Sunday 20(A)

Old Testament thought:
My house will be called a house of prayer for all peoples.
(Isaiah 56.7)

Vocal prayer:
O God, be gracious and bless us
and let your face shed its light upon us.
So will your ways be known upon earth
and all nations learn your saving help.
    Let the peoples praise you, O God;
    let all the peoples praise you.
Let the nations be glad and exult
for you rule the world with justice.
With fairness you rule the peoples,
you guide the nations on earth.
    Let all the peoples praise you, O God;
    let all the peoples praise you.   (From Psalm 67)

Gospel: Matthew 15.21–28

St Matthew's catechesis on the Church continues. In line with the vision of Isaiah, who saw all nations ascending the mountain of God, our Lord made a prophetic gesture by setting out towards the pagan region of Tyre and Sidon. In the meantime his mission, according to God's plan, was restricted to those who were currently the covenanted people of God, that is the Jews. This mission had to be completed before the mission to the whole world could properly begin. For this reason, therefore, when asked by the Canaanite woman to heal her daughter, Jesus stated that he had been sent only to the 'lost sheep of the house of Israel', and seemed reluctant to grant her request; but the incident ended with his granting the woman's request and healing her daughter, an act prophetic of what would happen after Pentecost.

The motive of the Twelve in wanting Jesus to answer the woman's prayer was simply to be rid of her. It was they, not Jesus, who thought that the children's bread should not ever be given to dogs – i.e. Gentiles. Quoting these words, Jesus was directing irony at the apostles. The woman by her reply showed not only sharp-wittedness, which Jesus appreciated, but faith. She had bothered to come out from the pagan region and crossed into the holy land of the covenant – symbolic of what all nations would have to do in future – and hailed Jesus as 'Lord'. Her great faith epitomized the faith that in future would be the key for all mankind to the kingdom of heaven.

Sunday 21(A)

Old Testament thought:
I shall drive him like a peg into a firm place.

(Isaiah 22.23)

Vocal prayer:
I will bless the Lord at all times,
his praise always on my lips;
in the Lord my soul shall make its boast.
The humble shall hear and be glad.
Glorify the Lord with me.
Together let us praise his name.
I sought the Lord and he answered me;
from all my terrors he set me free.
Look towards him and be radiant;
let your faces not be abashed.
This poor man called; the Lord heard him
and rescued him from all his distress.

(From Psalm 34)

Gospel: Matthew 16.13–20

St Matthew's Gospel continues to teach about the Church that is to be. The liturgy for today begins with an Old Testament reading that tells of the deposition of an unreliable major-domo in the royal household and his replacement by a worthier man. The major-domo kept the key to the royal apartments, having authority to admit to, or exclude from, the king's presence. He is likened also to a tent peg driven firmly into solid ground. No matter how grand the tent, without the peg it would have no stability.

This Old Testament image provides the background to Matthew's account of the commissioning of Simon Peter, who has already featured prominently in the storm incident, and who will retain his prominence until the end of this Gospel. Peter is to become the royal major-domo. He is given the key to the royal presence, the key to the kingdom of heaven; he is the tent peg upon which the stability of the edifice – the Church – depends. He is not the Church, but without him the Church would soon become an insecure habitation.

To these Old Testament images Jesus added another. He invented a completely new name for Simon – Peter, meaning 'Rock'. This image is even more powerful than the Old Testament images, and is more modern, for today we live in houses. Peter is not the whole building – many items are needed besides what he represents – but nothing else can endure unless it rests firmly upon him and the apostles, who are sacramentally united with him.

Sunday 22(A)

Old Testament thought:
The word of the Lord has meant for me insult,
    derision, all day long.   (Jeremiah 20.7)

Vocal prayer:
    For you my soul is thirsting, O Lord my God.
O God, you are my God, for you I long;
for you my soul is thirsting.
My body pines for you
like a dry, weary land without water.
So I gaze on you in the sanctuary
to see your strength and your glory.
For your love is better than life,
my lips will speak your praise.
    For you my soul is thirsting, O Lord my God.

                                        (From Psalm 63)

Gospel: Matthew 16.21–7

Peter at last understood that Jesus, son of Man, was also the Son of God, but when Jesus announced that he would have to suffer and die in Jerusalem, Peter did not understand; he took Jesus aside and remonstrated with him for talking such nonsense. By his reaction Peter betrayed that he shared much the same notion as the crowd, who expected the Messiah to liberate Israel from Roman rule and bring them political power. Peter had failed to see that the glorious Son of David and the Suffering Servant of the Lord were identical; in fact the divinity of the Messiah only confirmed his belief that the Messiah could not possible suffer.

Jesus not only corrected Peter's misconception: he rebuked him. 'Get behind me Satan! You are an obstacle in my path, because the way you think is not God's way but man's.' The mention of Satan can be seen as an allusion to our Lord's own temptations in the wilderness, for all of these temptations were aimed at enticing Jesus to gain power and influence by worldly means: providing material well-being (bread from stones), gaining popularity by compromising with evil (worshipping Satan), impressing people by supernatural or magical power (jumping unharmed from the pinnacle of the Temple). Peter's conception of the kingdom of Christ was exposed as tainted with this very fault. He was thinking in the way that unregenerate men and women think. And so Jesus prefixed his rebuke with the command: 'Get behind me!', which meant: 'Imitate me and not the way of the world!'

Just as the redemption of mankind had to be accomplished through our Lord's bodily suffering and death in perfect obedience to the will of God the Father, and not by extraordinary divine intervention, so the task he has assigned to his disciples has to be accomplished by effort and suffering and not through power. His disciples must follow him by taking up their particular crosses. There is, however, a cross which is common to all. Every disciple follows Christ by obeying the Ten Commandments and the moral teaching our Lord has bequeathed to his Church, to be handed down through the Church's magisterium. For most of us, because of the imperfection of our nature, to do this is to lay down our life, a kind of dying. We all have to surrender our own will to the will of God, just as in the Gethsemane Jesus said: 'Not my will but thy will be done.'

Sunday 23(A)

Old Testament thought:
Son of man, I have appointed you as sentry
　　to the House of Israel.
When you hear a word from my mouth,
　　warn them in my name.　　　　　　(Ezekiel 33.7)

Vocal prayer:
　O that today you would listen to his voice!
　Harden not your hearts.
Come in; let us bow and bend low;
let us kneel before the God who made us,
for he is our God and we the people who belong to
　　his pasture,
the flock that is led by his hand.
　O that today you would listen to his voice!
　Harden not your hearts.　　　　　　(From Psalm 95)

Gospel: Matthew 18.15–20

'Where two or three meet in my name, I shall be there with them.' This is not a general statement about our Lord's presence with his worshipping community, but applies specifically to the Church when assembled to administer discipline – that is to bind and loose.

Binding and loosing becomes necessary in cases of grave sin. 'If you brother does something wrong, go and have it out with him alone.' The person called upon to remonstrate with the wrong-doer may be the person wronged or simply one who knows of the other's sin. In either case the matter must be dealt with in private, in secret, for the wrong-doer has a right to his good name. If private remonstration fails a small number of others may be enlisted to help; if this fails then the matter must be drawn to the attention of the whole Church, that is of the local Church. If the offender remains unrepentant he must be excluded from the eucharistic fellowship. The object of such drastic action is to save the offender and also to preserve the good name of the Church, for the sin of any member brings the Church into ill-repute. Jesus told the disciples that when this kind of disciplinary action has to be taken, God the Father will uphold the decision of the Church. In these instructions given by our Lord we have the germ of the sacrament of penance. The precise ways in which this sacrament has come to be administered from time to time all embody the principles laid down by our Lord and recorded in St Matthew's Gospel.

The purpose of exclusion from the eucharistic fellowship was not to cut anyone off for ever, but so that such discipline might assist his eventual repentance and return into full communion with the Church. In the early centuries repentant sinners, especially those whose sin had caused public scandal, were reconciled publicly. After several months of penance they would be received back into communion by the bishop.

Today we are more concerned with sins that are not known to the public at large, but which on account of their gravity cause automatic self-excommunication, and which, because they have offended God and harmed the Church require not only repentance but also public reconciliation of the sinner. Such reconciliation is effected through the sacrament of penance which, while safe-guarding the sinner's right to his good name by the seal of confession, is at the same time a public act because the priest represents the Church. Confessing to him the peni-tent is confessing to the Church, to which our Lord gave this power to bind and to loose. With sacramental absolu-tion comes loosing from the bonds of sin.

Sunday 24(A)

Old Testament thought:
Forgive your neighbour the hurt he does you,
and when you pray, your sins will be forgiven.
If a man nurses anger against another,
can he then demand compassion from the Lord?

(Ecclesiasticus 28.2–3)

Vocal prayer:
My soul give thanks to the Lord,
all my being, bless his holy name.
My soul, give thanks to the Lord
and never forget all his blessings.
It is he who forgives all your guilt,
who heals every one of your ills,
who redeems your life from the grave,
who crowns you with love and compassion.
For as the heavens are high above the earth
so strong is his love for those who fear him.
As far as the east is from the west
so far does he remove our sins.

(From Psalm 103)

Gospel: Matthew 18.21–35

The obligation of men and women to forgive one another their sins was clearly acknowledged in the book of Ecclesiasticus, one of the last of the Wisdom books to be written (*c*. 190 BC). Our Lord Jesus, who is the Wisdom of God made flesh, affirmed this obligation even more insistently and explained why it is so fundamental to the life of the Church.

The old law had permitted revenge, but forbade unrestrained vendetta. It was to be proportionate revenge: 'an eye for an eye, a tooth for a tooth.' Our Lord, however, taught that all revenge must be set aside. Intensifying the light that had already shone in the late Wisdom literature, our Lord developed this theme, in particular in the parable recorded by St Matthew.

The forgiveness of which our Lord speaks is both reconciliation between estranged individuals, and also the more public reconciliation that is given sacramentally by the Church to an individual who by serious sin has forfeited the right to remain within the worshipping community. The latter is implied by the fact that it was Peter, so recently given the power to bind and loose, who asked the question: 'How often must I forgive my brother?'

Our Lord's reply made use of the symbolic perfect number seven. The Greek can be translated: 'seventy-seven' or 'seventy times seven', either way it is meant to convey the idea of an infinite number. The parable then explains the reason why forgiveness may not set itself limits. The sum owed by the first debtor amounted to £10,000,000 in comparison to about £15 owed him by his fellow-servant.

The enormous debt cancelled by the master represents the debt of original sin owed by all men and women to God the Creator. Compared with this the paltry debts we owe each other are laughable. Thankfulness to God for his limitless loving kindness ought to engender in all of us a generous and joyful compassion and mercy to all mankind.

Sunday 25(A)

Old Testament thought:
The heavens are as high above the earth
as my ways are above your ways,
my thoughts above your thoughts.   (Isaiah 55.8–9)

Vocal prayer:
    The Lord is close to all who call him.
The Lord is kind and full of compassion,
slow to anger, abounding in love.
How good is the Lord to all,
compassionate to all his creatures.
The Lord is just in all his ways
and loving in all his deeds.
He is close to all who call him,
who call on him from their hearts.
    The Lord is close to all who call him.

(From Psalm 145)

Gospel: Matthew 20.1–6

This parable was not meant by our Lord to provide a model for employment policy or wage structures; it is not about how the kingdoms of this world ought to be ordered, but about the principles upon which the kingdom of God is founded.

With this very simple story Jesus exposed the self-righteousness of many of the Jewish leaders who assumed that their membership of a people with whom God had made a covenant, their instruction by the prophets, and their detailed observance of the law of Moses gave them an exclusive and incontestable claim upon membership of the everlasting kingdom of God.

These leaders of the Jewish nation, satiated with self-esteem, are represented in the parable by the men hired at dawn; the pagan nations – all of mankind outside the old covenant – are represented by the labourers hired at intervals later. Our Lord was declaring very clearly, in contradiction to the popular Pharisaical view, that all men and women are potential members of the everlasting kingdom of God – and that the moral score that people acquire is not what gains them admission to this kingdom. Entry into God's kingdom, reception into eternal life is gained only through our heavenly Father's compassion, by his invitation.

The fault of the Pharisaical leaders – the men hired at dawn – was not their keeping of the law, for our Lord never encouraged carelessness in this regard, but their deep-seated conviction that their righteousness gave them a claim upon a place in God's kingdom. None of us is ever owed anything by God, it is we who owe him everything.

Sunday 26(A)

Old Testament thought:
When the sinner renounces his sin to become law-abiding
and honest, he deserves to live.   (Ezekiel 18.27)

Vocal prayer:
Lord, make me know your ways.
Lord, teach me your paths.
Make me walk in your truth, and teach me:
for you are God my saviour.
Remember your mercy, Lord,
and the love you have shown from of old.
Do not remember the sins of my youth.
In your love remember me,
because of your goodness, O Lord.
The Lord is good and upright.
He shows the path to those who stray,
he guides the humble in the right path;
he teaches his way to the poor.   (Psalm 25.4–9)

Gospel: Matthew 21.28–32

This parable, like the parable of the workers in the vineyard, was addressed to the religious leaders of the Jews. On the surface it makes the straightforward statement that repentance – the first son's thinking better of his disobedience – is most pleasing to God, and a precondition of a person's being received into the kingdom of God.

The mention of John the Baptist invites us to probe deeper. John had accused the religious leaders of being a 'brood of vipers'. In this parable Jesus picks up the theme that John had introduced on the banks of the Jordan, and asserts that gross sinners will make their way into the kingdom of God sooner than the religious leaders. These sinners are represented in the parable by the son who at first rebelled but later did go and do his father's bidding. The chief priests and elders of the people are represented by the son who said he would carry out his father's wishes but in fact did not. We can understand the first son's frame of mind fairly easily and rejoice with him in the knowledge that our heavenly Father too rejoices when we repent of wrong-doing and turn back to him. But what do we learn from the behaviour of the second son? The mind-set of the second son is what characterized the self-righteous religious leaders of our Lord's day. By meticulously observing the details of the Mosaic law they imagined that they were serving God, but they were deluding themselves, for their heart was not in the Lord's service. They may have been physically in the Lord's vineyard but their labour was forced labour.

This parable is not so much a warning to us to avoid direct contradiction of God's commandments as an exhortation to be on the look out for the self-deception which enables us to offer mere lip-service to God, by practising outward forms of devotion that express no love for our Father in heaven. This parable is very economical with words, but with inspired imagination we may see in the first son's change of heart a response to his father's love, for we cannot but be reminded of the other parable of two sons, one of whom was moved to repentance when he called to mind his father's goodness.

Sunday 27(A)

Old Testament thought:

What could I have done for my vineyard that I
    have not done?

I expected it to yield grapes. Why did it yield
    sour grapes instead?   (Isaiah 5.4)

Vocal prayer:

God of hosts, turn again, we implore,

look down from heaven and see.

Visit this vine and protect it,

the vine your right hand has planted.

And we shall never forsake you again:

give us life that we may call upon your name.

God of hosts, bring us back;

let your face shine on us and we shall be saved.

(From Psalm 80)

Gospel: Matthew 21.33–43

The song of the vineyard, contained in the book of Isaiah, prepares us to hear our Lord's parable. In Isaiah's poem the vineyard is the house of Israel. The Lord God created that vineyard out of love, and provided it with protection and all the means of producing good fruit, but it failed to do so, and so the Lord let it go to waste. The house of Israel had disobeyed God's commandments and failed to produce the fruits of sanctifying grace, and so the Lord, at various times, withdrew from it all the benefits it had formerly enjoyed.

Our Lord's parable is an adaptation of this Old Testament poem. Our Lord concentrates attention upon those who cultivate the vineyard, whom he now describes as its tenants. The vineyard itself is not unproductive but when the grape harvest is ready the tenants refuse to give it up to the owner. This detail points to the fault underlying disobedience to God's law: mankind's claiming to have the same rights as his Creator.

The two separate delegations of servants represent respectively the early prophets sent to recall the people of Israel to observance of the law, and the post-exilic prophets sent to perform the same function. All of the prophets had suffered at the hands of the religious establishment, just as Jesus, represented in the parable by the son sent to make a final appeal to the tenants, was to suffer death at the hands of that same establishment.

The last detail in the parable is a prophecy of the passion and death of Christ. In a footnote to this parable Matthew tells us that 'the chief scribes and pharisees realized he was speaking about them, but though they would have liked to arrest him they were afraid of the crowds, who looked on him as a prophet.'

The concluding scene of our Lord's parable is more elaborate than the end of Isaiah's poem. In the poem the vineyard is simply let go to waste; in the parable the vineyard is leased out to new tenants, who are all the pagan nations of the earth, whom the leaders of the scribes and

Pharisees regarded as ineligible for membership of the kingdom of God. Our Lord described these new tenants as 'a people who will produce its (the vine's) fruit.' The mere fact that the new tenants have been installed does not however guarantee that they will behave any better than the former tenants had done. They too would be obliged to yield up the fruit in due season.

We are reminded of the great parable of the vine in which our Lord speaks of the disciple having to remain as a fruit-bearing branch in the vine, that is always receiving sap from the vine-stock. The parable of the tenants in the vineyard is related also to the parable of the talents, which tells how two servants produced a fine return on the money entrusted to them, and how one of the servants merely buried his talent and produced no profit at all. A terrible judgement fell upon that man.

At our baptism the Lord endows each of us with spiritual gifts, and it is on these gifts, even more than on our natural gifts, that our Lord wishes to see a good return when he comes to judge us. These gifts or virtues fall roughly into three groups: purity of heart; a humble and penitential frame of mind; the spirit of mercy and compassion. When our Lord comes on the Day of Judgement he will hope to see in each of us a great increase of these virtues, manifested in the blessings their exercise has effected in the world around us, for the virtues are given not for our own enjoyment but as the instruments, the energy, by which we are enabled to mediate the creative and redemptive love of God to all mankind.

Not only has our Lord endowed each of us at baptism with virtues that are no less than a share in the richness of his own wisdom and love, but he has generously provided for their nourishment in us through the sacraments of the Church and the privilege of prayer in the name of his Son. There is absolutely no excuse for us therefore if we fail to yield up to him on his coming a rich harvest of fruit from the vineyard in which he has installed us.

St Paul's exhortation in today's second reading provides

an appropriate conclusion to meditation upon the Gospel parable. 'Fill your minds with everything that is true, everything that is noble, everything that is good and pure, everything that we love and honour, and everything that can be thought virtuous or worthy of praise' (Philippians 4.8).

Sunday 28(A)

Old Testament thought:
On this mountain, the Lord of hosts will prepare
  for all peoples
a banquet of rich food, a banquet of fine wines,
of food rich and juicy, of fine strained wines.

(Isaiah 25.6)

Vocal prayer:
You have prepared a banquet for me
in the sight of my foes.
My head you have anointed with oil;
my cup is overflowing.
Surely goodness and kindness shall follow me
all the days of my life.
In the Lord's own house shall I dwell
for ever and ever.

(From Psalm 23)

Gospel: Matthew 22.1–14

The three parables (all set in vineyards) which we have read over the past three weeks, are about the attitude of mind and heart, that fits men and women for membership in the kingdom of God; the parable read on Sunday 28 recapitulates much of the teaching contained in these parables, and adds some important new material.

The people who decline the invitation to the wedding feast are the self-righteous leaders whom we have met already in other parables, and whom our Lord was encountering in real life. It would have hurt their pride to accept an invitation into the kingdom, for they thought they had a right to be in it. But the parable tells us also that they deserve punishment for their refusal to accept. This sin is no less than the unforgivable sin, for it is a self-condemnation through rejection of God's gift of grace. God's grace is freely given but it has to be freely accepted.

Those who are then invited in place of the alleged friends of the king are the tax-collectors and prostitutes, all of the motley crowd who make no pretension of being worthy. Their grateful and joyful acceptance of the invitation speaks of a totally different mentality from that of the scribes and Pharisees: they accept the fact that their only chance of getting into the feast (the kingdom) is if they are invited. The first group, the originally invited, are punished for their pride, the second group, the sinners, are rewarded for their humility and penitence.

The little appendix to the parable is really a new parable. The guests have now entered the banqueting hall; the king notices that one of them is not wearing the customary ceremonial wedding garment; this man is thrown out. It is not enough to accept the invitation. Having accepted and entered the place of rejoicing the guests are expected to assume a new lifestyle. The application of the parable is very simple. We who have received forgiveness and taken our place at the Lord's banquet, the Holy Eucharist, which is a foreshadowing of heavenly marriage feast of the Lamb, must produce the fruits of repentance (cf. the parable of the vineyard tenants). We have been redeemed by God's grace, but we must persevere in good works.

This parable is brought to mind at baptisms when a white garment is given to the infant or adult accompanied by the admonition to preserve their Christian dignity, of which the garment is the sign, until they come to the heavenly banquet. The same symbolism is used at funerals when a white pall is placed over the coffin as it leaves the church, with the same symbolism.

Sunday 29(A)

Old Testament thought:
I am the Lord, unrivalled, there is no other God
    beside me.   (Isaiah 45.5)

Vocal prayer:
Give the Lord, you families of the peoples,
give the Lord glory and power,
give the Lord the glory of his name.
Bring an offering and enter his courts.

Worship the Lord in his temple.
O earth, tremble before him.
Proclaim to the nations: 'God is king.'
He will judge the peoples in fairness.

                              (From Psalm 96)

Gospel: Matthew 22.15–21

The Pharisees laid a trap for Jesus. They asked him if it was right for Jews to pay the Roman poll tax. Were he to answer 'Yes' he would lose the support of most Jews, who complained that these pagans had no right to tax God's own land and people; were he to say 'No' he would make himself liable to arrest and trial as a fomenter of rebellion. The questioners were insincere, having no real interest in what Jesus would say, for they despised him as a teacher. In addressing him as 'teacher' they were in fact sneering at him.

Jesus, knowing their insincerity, did not answer directly. He put them on the spot by asking for the coin with which the tax was paid – a denarius. By this action and his reply he was saying in effect: 'I haven't got this coin, but you have, which means that you are quite happy to make use of the emperor's coins and enjoy the civic rights and facilities which the Roman state gives you. You ought therefore to pay him his due.' Then he added: 'But see to it that you give to God what you owe him.'

This final exhortation is of a piece with the message of the parable about giving to the lord of the vineyard what the vineyard and its tenants owe him. The message for us and for all time is that it is obvious that we owe material dues to the civil authorities, for we all make us of what society has to offer, but it is much more important that we reverence and obey our Creator.

Sunday 30(A)

Old Testament thought:
You must not molest the stranger or oppress him,
for you lived as strangers in the land of Egypt.

(Exodus 22.21)

Vocal prayer:
  I love you Lord, my strength.
  I love you Lord, my strength,
my rock, my fortress, my saviour.
My God is the rock where I take refuge;
my shield, my mighty help, my stronghold.
The Lord is worthy of all praise,
when I call I am saved from my foes,.
  I love you Lord, my strength.   (From Psalm 18)

Gospel: Matthew 22.34–40

Again the Pharisees addressed Jesus as 'Teacher', and again they spoke with sarcasm. They did not really consider him to be a teacher, for they questioned him, not so as to learn from him, but to lure him into contradicting the Law of Moses or else say something that would lose him the support of the people.

The reply Jesus gave allowed of no debate or comment. He simply quoted a verse from the book of Deuteronomy which by his time had become the foundational prayer of Jewish piety – as it still is – the Shema – 'listen, Israel'. The words of this text go deeper than any of the particular precepts of the Law. The command: 'You must love the Lord your God with all your heart and with all your soul, and with all your mind', was one that his questioners accepted as the foundation of the Law. In giving this answer Jesus did not introduce discussion on relative merits of particular laws, thus avoiding possible controversy.

In the addition that Jesus made to this basic command he alluded, however, to the rabbinic practice of distinguishing 'heavy' laws from 'light' laws. He asserted that the command to love God, and the command to love one's neighbour, were equally 'heavy'. The love of God is the absolute foundation of true piety, but if that love is genuine it shows itself in love of neighbour. The two loves are the two faces of one coin.

Sunday 31(A)

Old Testament thought:
Do not speak and speak with haughty words,
let not arrogance come from your mouth.

(1 Samuel 2.3)

Vocal prayer:
O Lord, my heart is not proud
nor haughty my eyes.
I have not gone after things too great
nor marvels beyond me.
Truly I have set my soul
in silence and peace.
A weaned child on its mother's breast,
even so is my soul.

(From Psalm 131)

Gospel: Matthew 23.1–12

The leaders of the people ceased arguing with Jesus. 'From that day on no one dared ask him any further questions' (Matthew 22.46). Now it was his turn to take the offensive. Today we learn how he denounced the scribes and Pharisees because, while claiming the authority of Moses, they did not practise what they preached. He complained also of the way they burdened the simple people with fussy outward precepts which had no real connection with true morality; and he described how the scribes and Pharisees made an outward show of their piety by wearing on their arms and foreheads boxes containing parchments bearing verses of the Law, and by wearing tassels on their cloaks – symbols of the Law. These objects got bigger and bigger as they strained to show off their piety.

Jesus pointed out too how these pompous people liked to be given prominence in the community and to be addressed as 'Rabbi' or 'Abba'. It was not the word 'teacher' or the word 'father' to which Jesus objected; he condemned both those who used the titles and those who accepted their use when that was done obsequiously.

In the Church there are teachers, but no teacher must think that he teaches in his own name: he is a channel for the teaching of the Teacher, Christ. In the early Church the Aramaic word 'Abba' became used exclusively to denote the Father of the Lord's Prayer. In English today that is not so; we would render 'Abba' by the whole phrase, 'Our Father who art in heaven'. The word 'father' for us is certainly not an obsequious, but a familial, title, and hence perfectly acceptable.

Sunday 32(A)

Old Testament thought:
Wisdom is bright and does not grow dim.
By those who love her she is readily seen,
and found by those who look for her.
She herself walks about
looking for those who are worthy of her.

(Wisdom 6.12; 16)

Vocal prayer:
O God, you are my God, for you I long;
for you my soul is thirsting.
My body pines for you
like a dry, weary land without water.
So I gaze on you in the sanctuary
to see your strength and your glory.
For your love is better than life,
my lips will speak your praise.   (From Psalm 63)

Gospel: Matthew 25.1–13

Prayer is our seeking for the Wisdom that is God; but Wisdom is already seeking for us. We, therefore, for our part must be alert and in a fit state to respond to Wisdom when he comes to invite us into his kingdom. Our seeking him is equivalent to keeping ourselves in a state of loving expectation of his coming.

St John calls the Wisdom of God his Word, and tells us that this Word became flesh and dwelt among us. The Word is one also with the Love of God. That Love came down to us and seeks us out in several ways, and on every occasion we must be like the wise bridesmaids who never let their lamps run out of oil. Waiting for our Lord, our lives must be for ever bright with virtue.

Our Lord, the Bridegroom, will come to meet us on the great day of Judgement; but he will come also in particular judgement on the day of our death; and he comes too during our lives in many events and encounters, when we have to make decisions and choose between right and wrong; he comes to us in times of private prayer and in the corporate prayer of the Church, when we meet him in the Liturgy of the Word and in his Real Presence in the Eucharist.

For any of these meetings with the Lord we must be prepared, and an effective method of preparation is to develop the habit of meditative prayer. We train ourselves to read the Scriptures and become acquainted in detail with our Lord's life and teaching, and to become preoccupied with the things of his kingdom. If we constantly practise the presence of our Lord in this way we will not be disconcerted or left outside when he comes to invite us into his heavenly wedding feast.

Sunday 33(A)

Old Testament thought:
She keeps good watch on the conduct of her household,
no bread of idleness for her.
Her sons stand up and proclaim her blessed,
her husband, too, sings her praise:
Many women have done admirable things,
but you surpass them all.

(Proverbs 31.27–9)

Vocal prayer:
My soul proclaims the greatness of the Lord
and my spirit exults in God my Saviour;

because he has looked upon his lowly handmaid.

Yes, from this day forward all generations will call
me blessed,

for the Almighty has done great things for me.

Holy is his name.   (Luke 1.46–49)

Gospel: Matthew 25.14–30

This parable stresses the responsibility of all people to use fully, to the glory of God, every gift that has been given them. This applies not only to natural gifts, but also to those supernatural gifts which nourish a life of virtue. In this parable the cloud of judgement hangs over the scene. The servant who produced no yield from his single talent was severely punished by the removal of his talent and exclusion from his master's presence. For the Christian, not to produce fruits of the Spirit results in the withdrawal of the Spirit, which means severance from God.

The reading from the book of Proverbs which prepares us for the Gospel today is not just a piece of homely, domestic morality, but speaks of the Daughter of Sion, the personification of Israel, the Bride of the King who was to come, a personification indeed of the Church. Today's parable therefore is not merely an exhortation to the individual believer but an admonition to the Church as a whole to fulfil the task of the perfect wife and mother: to keep 'good watch on the conduct of her household' and to 'open her arms to the needy'. It is the Church who possesses the means of supplying spiritual nourishment to all of her members, so that they may produce the fruits of the Spirit and merit the commendation 'Well done, good and faithful servant, come and join in your master's happiness.'

Sunday 34(A): The Feast of Christ the Universal King

Old Testament thought:
The Lord says this:
I am going to look after my flock myself and keep all of it
   in view.
I shall rescue them from wherever they have scattered.

(Ezekiel 34.11–12)

Vocal prayer:
The Lord is my shepherd;
there is nothing I shall want.
Fresh and green are the pastures
where he gives me repose.
Near restful waters he leads me,
to revive my drooping spirit.

(From Psalm 23)

Gospel: Matthew 25.31–46

In biblical times Middle Eastern kings were tyrants, but the Israelites regarded their king as a shepherd who cared for his people. Their kings did not always live up to this ideal, but at the end of their history came One who did: Jesus, Son of God and Son of Mary. He gave his life for his people – the whole human race.

His humility, his total self-emptying did not, however, take from him the right to come again in glory to judge all of mankind. Today we meditate on his second coming as judge. In his great apocalyptic discourse Jesus announced very clearly the principles by which he would judge. As he himself had emptied himself of divine privilege and given himself unreservedly for all, so he would judge all people according to the measure in which they had given themselves in the care of others, especially of the poor and the afflicted.

He asserted – to the amazement of even the righteous – that serving the poor and afflicted was equivalent to serving him. The reason why this is so is because he, the true Son of God, had been made man. 'The Word became flesh and lived among us' (John 1.14); and so he dwells mysteriously in every suffering human being.

To qualify for eternal life we must empty ourselves in the service of the poor, as he did. Correct belief is important, but salvific only if it guides us into the imitation of Christ; faith saves us, but faith is true only if it flows into love.

SUNDAYS IN ORDINARY TIME, CYCLE B

Sunday 13(B)

Old Testament thought:
Death was not God's doing,
he takes no pleasure in the extinction of the living.
To be – for this he created all.   (Wisdom 1.13–14)

Vocal prayer:
Preserve me God, I take refuge in you.
I say to the Lord: 'You are my God.'
O Lord, it is you who are my portion and cup;
it is you yourself who are my prize.
I will bless the Lord who gives me counsel,
who even at night directs my heart.
I keep the Lord ever in my sight:
since he is at my right hand, I shall stand firm.
And so my heart rejoices, my soul is glad;
even my body shall rest in safety.
For you will not leave my soul among the dead;
nor let your beloved know decay.   (From Psalm 16)

Gospel: Mark 5.21–43

Two narratives are contained in today's Gospel reading. One is enclosed within the other, suggesting that we ought to observe how they are related. Even so, we may meditate on each separately. The miracle of the raising of Jairus's daughter is a real miracle but, as in the case of the calming of the storm, it has a catechetical dimension and contains a message for every age.

Jairus asked Jesus to lay his hands on the child so that she might be made well and live. For the early Christian readers of Mark's Gospel the words used for 'make well' and 'live' meant also to be 'saved' and to 'have eternal life'. By this miracle Jesus declared his power to grant salvation (forgiveness) and victory over death, that is to give eternal life.

Commanding the girl to arise, Jesus used a word that is used also of his own resurrection; and when he said that she was not dead but only sleeping he affirmed that death is only a sleep from which the believer will be awakened in the resurrection. Only Peter and James and John were present at this miracle as they would be at the transfiguration, when Jesus manifested his glory and gave a preview of his resurrection. The purpose of this miracle is most of all to reveal Jesus's power to save men and women from sin and death and bring them into eternal life.

The same applies to the cure of the woman with the persistent haemorrhage. She had heard reports about Jesus. The Greek used here is that used in the early Church to denote hearing about the resurrection of Jesus. The woman's malady was considered to cause ritual uncleanness – hence her fear and trembling, and her desire not to be noticed when she touched another person. Her cure was a sign of purification, of salvation. Our Lord's declaration: 'Your faith has made you well' was equivalent to: 'Your faith has won you salvation.' The emphasis on the woman's touching Jesus could be a hint of the Christian's need for the Real Presence of Christ in the Eucharist or of the sacraments in general.

These miracles teach us that in every age Jesus is able to grant salvation and eternal life to all who worship him in faith and loving obedience, accepting all the means of salvation provided by his Body, the Church.

Sunday 14(B)

Old Testament thought:
Never forget how you provoked the Lord your God.
From the day you came out of the land of Egypt you have been rebels against the Lord.

(Deuteronomy 9.7)

Vocal prayer:
Save me, God! The water is already up to my neck!
I have stepped into deep water
and the waters are washing over me.
Pull me out of this swamp; let me sink no further,
let me escape those who hate me,
save me from deep water!
Do not let the waves wash over me,
do not let the deep swallow me
or the Pit close its mouth on me.   (From Psalm 69)

Gospel: Mark 6.1–6

Rejection of Jesus is a dominant theme in Mark's Gospel. From today's reading we learn that Jesus was rejected even by his own townsfolk. On this visit he was accompanied by his disciples, indicating that he came in his role as the Messiah, and so it was as Messiah that the people were rejecting him. Declaring himself publicly in this way as more than a prophet, Jesus placed himself none the less in the line of the prophets who in the past had suffered rejection and persecution, thus associating himself with the image of the Suffering Servant of the Lord. The people of Nazareth were pleased to count him as one of their own, in his role as wonder-worker, but as for his being the Messiah, that was a different matter. St John tells us that he came to his own and his own did not accept him; St Mark suggests that they rejected him precisely because he was one of themselves. '"This is the carpenter's son, surely, the son of Mary, the brother of James and Joset and Jude and Simon? His sisters, too, are they not here with us?" And they would not accept him.'

They expected the Messiah to be magnificent and powerful, one in whose splendour they could share. This man was just one of themselves. To follow one who radiated humility and spoke of suffering offered them no prospect of advancement. Down the centuries the triumphalism of the people of Nazareth asserts itself repeatedly – even in the Church.

Sunday 15(B)

Old Testament thought:
Amaziah the priest said to Amos:
'Go away, seer, get back to the land of Judah,
we want no more prophesying in Bethel;
this is the royal sanctuary, the national temple.'

(Amos 7.12–13)

Vocal prayer:
I will hear what the Lord has to say,
a voice that speaks of peace,
peace for his people.
His help is near for those who fear him
and his glory will dwell in our land.
Mercy and faithfulness have met;
justice and peace have embraced.
Faithfulness shall spring from the earth
and justice look down from heaven.
The Lord will make us prosper
and our earth shall yield its fruit.
Justice shall march before him
and peace shall follow his steps.   (From Psalm 85)

Gospel: Mark 6.7–13

The prophet Amos learned that prosperity and vested interests made people resistant to his preaching of God's word. The northern kingdom of Israel had prospered, but the wealthy were oppressing the weak. The priest in charge of the royal chapel told Amos to go home to the southern province of Judah and preach there.

In Nazareth Jesus had been rebuffed by his own people. Now he turned towards the wider world; first he preached in Galilee which was still Jewish territory; then in his commissioning of the Twelve to go and preach repentance we see the foreshadowing of his mission to all nations. The stress on repentance suggests that the preaching of the kingdom could be fully carried out only after the resurrection. For the time being the Twelve were to prepare people for entry into the kingdom.

The fundamental commission given to the Twelve was to cast out unclean spirits. According to Jewish belief unclean spirits manifested their power in physical and mental disorder; but we should understand the casting out of unclean spirits in a wider sense. The power of Jesus, coming to us through the preaching and the sacraments of the Church, is a power over all that is evil, however it manifests itself.

We ought constantly to assess the motives which control our actions: which impulses are from God, which from our own selfish desires? We try to root out our serious sins, which come from the spirit of evil, by repentance and seeking sacramental absolution, but we must try also through healthy self-knowledge to remove the residual sources of evil-doing which, like the rhizomes of couch grass in our gardens, lurk in the soil of our being.

Sunday 16(B)

Old Testament thought:
The remnant of my flock I myself will gather from all the
countries where I have dispersed them.

(Jeremiah 23.3)

Vocal prayer:
The Lord is my shepherd;
there is nothing I shall want.
Fresh and green are the pastures
where he gives me repose.
Near restful waters he leads me,
to revive my drooping spirit.
He guides me along the right path;
he is true to his name.

If I should walk in the valley of darkness
no evil would I fear.
You are there with your crook and your staff;
with these you give me comfort.

You have prepared a banquet for me
in the sight of my foes.
My head you have anointed with oil;
my cup is overflowing.

Surely goodness and kindness shall follow me
all the days of my life.
In the Lord's own house shall I dwell
for ever and ever.

(Psalm 23)

Gospel: Mark 6.30–34

After their missionary journey the Twelve are named 'apostles', the only time that Mark uses the word. They are exhausted, and so Jesus takes them off to a lonely place to rest, but also for private instruction. Not just official ministers of the Church, but all Christians find it necessary to pause, rest, and pray after spiritual effort – every day. Discipleship, that is being a learner, is the foundation of effective apostleship – being a worker for the kingdom of God.

This brief interlude introduces the celebrated scene of the feeding of the five thousand, the setting of which is the deserted place to which Jesus has gone with the Twelve. The occasion is also a time of instruction and prayer, a feeding with the Word by the Word. The human race, represented by the multitude, are hungry, that is ignorant, but seeking the truth, and already looking to Jesus, expecting to receive from him what they need. They are a flock as yet without a shepherd who can feed them and hold them together in unity. The introduction to the episode ends with Jesus beginning to teach them at some length. They have everything to learn.

Sunday 17(B)

Old Testament thought:
The prophet Elisha said: 'Give it to the people to eat, for
the Lord says this, "They will eat and have some left
over."'   (2 Kings 4.43)

Vocal prayer:
All your creatures shall thank you, O Lord,
and your friends shall repeat their blessing.
They shall speak of the glory of your reign
and declare your might, O Lord.

The eyes of all creatures look to you
and you give them their food in due time.
You open wide your hand,
grant the desires of all who live

The Lord is just in all his ways
and loving in all his deeds.
He is close to all who call on him,
who call on him from their hearts.   (From Psalm 145)

Gospel: John 6.1–15

The account of the feeding of the multitude in St John's Gospel introduces the theme of the Bread of Life, to which five Sundays are devoted. Before performing the miracle, Jesus had begun to teach 'at great length'; the teaching develops into a teaching about the Eucharist, and this is hinted by the statement that the feast of the Passover is approaching.

The concept of the Word of God is fundamental to the whole series of Gospel passages which we will read over the next five Sundays. To the Jew bread symbolized the Word of God. The manna in the desert was bread provided by God's creative act, by his Word. When Jesus was tempted by the Devil he said: 'Man does not live by bread alone, but by every word that proceeds from the mouth of God.' In the Old Testament the prophet Elisha had passed on God's command that the barley bread be multiplied, and God's word had accomplished this. Jesus himself commands the barley loaves to feed the multitude. He is more than a prophet, he is the Word. In considering this miracle we must, therefore, see first of all, that by it Jesus declared himself to be the Word by whom all was created.

The people failed to grasp this, thinking him to be a prophet like Elisha, who would satisfy their material needs, and so when they tried to acclaim him King he fled into the hills.

Sunday 18(B)

Old Testament thought:
On the surface of the desert was a thing delicate, powdery. The sons of Israel said, 'What is it?' Moses said: 'It is the bread that the Lord has given you to eat.'

(Exodus 16.14–15)

Vocal prayer:
The things we have heard and understood,
the things our fathers have told us,
we will tell to the next generation.
He commanded the clouds from above
and opened the gates of heaven.
He rained down manna for their food,
and gave them bread from heaven.
Mere men ate the bread of angels.
He sent them abundance of food.
He brought them to his holy land,
to the mountain which his right hand had won.

(From Psalm 78)

Gospel: John 6.24–35

The crowd are following Jesus because they want earthly food; they have not understood the meaning of the miracle. Jesus upbraids them and tells them that they ought to be seeking the food that gives them spiritual nourishment. Such is the food the Messiah brings. At this point Jesus says that the Father has 'set his seal' upon him, preparing the way for his affirmation that he is one with the Father. The crowd ask Jesus what they must do to please the Father; he tells them that they must believe in him; their response is to ask for a sign, further proof that they have misunderstood the sign proclaimed by the miracle. They compare Jesus unfavourably with Moses, who in the desert had given them bread from heaven. Jesus points out that it was not Moses who had given that bread and that in any case it was not 'bread from heaven' but only bodily sustenance. When Jesus begins to speak of the heavenly bread that will give life to the world they seem to show some desire to have this bread. Responding to their incipient faith Jesus declares that he is the true bread come down from heaven. He is the Word (symbolized by bread) through whom all things were created, and so is both giver and gift of the bread that nourishes eternal life.

Sunday 19(B)

Old Testament thought:
The angel of the Lord said: 'Get up and eat, otherwise the journey will be too much for you.' So he got up and ate, and walked for forty days and forty nights.

(1 Kings 19.7–8)

Vocal prayer:
Of the glorious Body telling,

O my tongue, its mysteries sing,

And the Blood, all price excelling,

Which the world's eternal King,

In a noble womb once dwelling,

Shed for the world's ransoming.

Word-made-flesh, by word he maketh

Bread his very Flesh to be;

Man in wine Christ's Blood partaketh:

And if senses fail to see,

Faith alone the true heart waketh

To behold the mystery.   (From the *Pange Lingua*)

Gospel: John 6.41–51

The audience were now beginning to grasp something of what Jesus was trying to teach them. Possibly they had begun to understand that he was claiming to be God's Word in a special sense. But how, they wondered, could he have come down from heaven? They knew that he came from Nazareth.

And now Jesus raises the big problem of why some people believe in him and others do not. The key to finding faith in Jesus, to believing that he truly is the Son of God, is found in the attitude to God the Father which has guided the person in the past. If his hearers had been listening attentively and obediently to the Father's voice, teaching them through the Law and the prophets, they would understand who Jesus is and would come to him. What Jesus said to these people he says to us also. Jesus then returned to the theme of the Bread of Life. The manna, as we noted, was only temporary food. Now Jesus gives the Word of God, which is food for eternal life, and he gives it through his own flesh, that is to say not just in his teaching but in a mysterious reality. The word 'flesh' has also an overtone of sacrifice.

Sunday 20(B)

Old Testament thought:
Wisdom says:
'Come and eat my bread,
drink the wine I have prepared!
Leave your folly and you will live,
walk in the ways of perception.   (Proverbs 9.5–6)

Vocal prayer:
How can I repay the Lord
for his goodness to me?
The cup of salvation I will raise;
I will call on the Lord's name.
O precious in the eyes of the Lord
is the death of his faithful.
Your servant, Lord, your servant am I;
you have loosened my bonds.
A thanksgiving sacrifice I make:
I will call on the Lord's name
My vows to the Lord I will fulfil
before all his people.   (From Psalm 116)

Gospel: John 6.51–58

The Gospel passage for today opens with a repetition of the ending of last Sunday's Gospel. This overlap draws our attention to the fact that, in his discourse on the Bread of Life, Jesus is reaching a climax, now moving from the notion of listening obediently to the Word of his teaching to the notion of communion with him by eating the sacrificed Word made flesh.

The audience immediately recoil at this thought; they think that Jesus is advocating some form of cannibalism. Jesus's first response to them is not to argue or clarify but simply to reiterate his assertion: 'if you do not eat the flesh of the Son of Man and drink his blood, you will not have life in you.' Conversely those who do so eat and drink will enjoy eternal life.

The full explanation of what our Lord meant comes in the Gospel for next Sunday; at this stage of his encounter with the people he gives only a clue by speaking of raising up on the last day those who have eaten and drunk his body and blood. Interpretation of what our Lord meant when he spoke of eating his flesh and drinking his blood is possible only in the context of resurrection.

Before concluding this section of his discourse, Jesus introduces the theme of his own substantial union with the Father. This union was not just through obedience to the Father's will but was a sharing in the substance of the Father. The same kind of substantial sharing has to come about between the believer and the Lord, accomplished through eating his flesh and drinking his blood. There has to be a physical union with the Son so that the believer can share in the life of the Father.

Sunday 21(B)

Old Testament thought:
The people answered: 'We have no intention of deserting
the Lord, and serving other gods! Was it not the Lord our
God who brought us and our ancestors out of the land of
Egypt, the house of slavery?'   (Joshua 24.16–17)

Vocal prayer:
I will bless the Lord at all times

his praise always on my lips;

in the Lord my soul shall make its boast.

The humble shall hear and be glad.

The Lord turns his face against the wicked

to destroy their remembrance from the earth.

The Lord turns his eyes to the just

and his ears to their appeal.

They call and the Lord hears and rescues them in all
  their distress.

The Lord is close to the broken-hearted;

those whose spirit is crushed he will save.

                                        (From Psalm 34)

Gospel: John 6.60–69

At this point in his discourse on the Bread of Life many of his followers deserted Jesus. The sticking point was what he had said about eating his flesh. 'This is intolerable language. How could anyone accept it?'

Jesus could have overcome their objection had he stated that he was speaking metaphorically. He could have explained his statement: 'The words I have spoken to you are spirit and they are life' by saying that eating his flesh meant simply hearing his words and believing them. But he gave no such explanation to reassure them. His answer was to relate his intolerable saying to his resurrection and ascension. 'What if you should see the Son of Man ascend to where he was before?' When we try to comprehend the mystery of eating his flesh and drinking his blood we ought to think of his transfigured body. The body that was raised to life by the Father through the power of the Holy Spirit. Jesus continued: 'It is the spirit that gives life, the flesh has nothing to offer', although he had said that to gain eternal life we must eat his flesh. He means that dead flesh has nothing to offer; it is not his dead body as it was on the Cross that we must eat but his body as it was after its resurrection. It is this body or, more correctly, his body, blood, soul, and divinity that we consume in the holy eucharist.

The report of our Lord's discourse on the Bread of Life ends with Peter's declaration of faith. Speaking for the Twelve he affirms their faith that Jesus is the Holy One of God. This faith enables them to accept all that he has said.

Sunday 22(B)

Old Testament thought:
Now, Israel, take note of the laws and customs that I teach
you today, and observe them, that you may have life.
(Deuteronomy 4.1)

Vocal prayer:
Lord, who shall dwell on your holy mountain?
He who walks without fault;
he who acts with justice,
and speaks the truth from his heart.
He who does no wrong to his brother,
who casts no slur on his neighbour,
who holds the godless in disdain,
but honours those who fear the Lord.
He who keeps his pledge, come what may;
who takes no interest on a loan,
and accepts no bribes against the innocent.
Such a man will stand firm for ever.

(From Psalm 15)

Gospel: Mark 7.1–8; 14–23

All three readings in today's liturgy tell of God's law. Deuteronomy insists that the law given through Moses is for ever valid and binding. St Paul echoed this thought in the mid-first century when he wrote: 'The law is sacred, and what it commands is sacred, just and good' (Romans 7.12). Most important, however, is the affirmation in Deuteronomy that keeping the law will lead to life.

The law is not an imposed burden but a gift of knowledge that enables mankind to find happiness; for the law is the law of our nature, and by keeping that law we become what we are meant to be.

In today's Gospel Jesus reproached the scribes and Pharisees for stressing trivial human regulations that distracted people from the weightier matters of human conduct. Keeping the law is difficult – for the spirit of disorder still works within us – and so people substitute their own pseudo-moral customs and make a great fuss about keeping these, for it is much easier to create a moral feel-good mentality in this way, than to seek God's grace to enable us to keep faithful to the genuine law that is designed to purify the heart from evil impulses to fornication, murder, theft, malice, envy, and pride.

Moral cleanness is acquired not by ritual washings, but by expelling from our hearts all that is contrary to the love of God and our neighbour. The law points the way to the true, selfless love in which we find the fullness of life.

Sunday 23(B)

Old Testament thought:
Then the eyes of the blind shall be opened, and the ears
of the deaf unsealed.   (Isaiah 35.5)

Vocal prayer:
It is the Lord who keeps faith for ever,
who is just to those who are oppressed.
It is he who gives bread to the hungry,
the Lord, who sets prisoners free.

It is the Lord who gives sight to the blind,
who raises up those who are bowed down,
the Lord who loves the just,
the Lord, who protects the stranger.

The Lord upholds the widow and orphan,
but thwarts the path of the wicked.
The Lord will reign for ever,
Zion's God, from age to age. Alleluia.

(From Psalm 146)

Gospel: Mark 7.31–37

The prophet Isaiah had foretold that when the Messiah came he would open the eyes of the blind and unseal the ears of the deaf. He foretold also that all nations would converge upon Zion to worship the one true God. By performing the particular miracle recorded in today's Gospel, Jesus fulfilled these prophecies and so declared that he was the Messiah, and he performed this miracle in pagan territory, in order to make clear that all mankind were to be welcomed into God's kingdom.

Putting the fingers into the ears and touching the tongue with spittle were gestures commonly used by Jewish and Greek healers in the time of Jesus. Jesus, however, also looked up to heaven so as to emphasize his intimacy with the Father. But the act of healing went further than the healing of this individual. Jesus was healing people, who had not received the word of God, and did not offer him true worship. By this miracle Jesus indicated that his people and all pagans will have their ears opened to the word of God and their tongues loosened in order to worship God in Spirit and in truth.

The miracle speaks to us too: our ears have been opened to hear God's word, and we must respond by offering God the worship that he desires. These facts are proclaimed in the ceremonies of our baptismal rite.

Jesus commanded the people to keep quiet about this miracle. He did not want to attract a following amongst those who were impressed only by the external aspect of his miracles, while failing to understand the sign he was giving.

Sunday 24(B)

Old Testament thought:
For my part, I made no resistance,
neither did I turn away.
I offered my back to those who struck me.

(Isaiah 50.5)

Vocal prayer:
I love the Lord for he has heard
the cry of my appeal;
for he turned his ear to me
in the day when I called him.
How gracious is the Lord and just;
our Lord has compassion.
The Lord protects the simple hearts;
I was helpless so he saved me.
He has kept my soul from death,
my eyes from tears,
and my feet from stumbling.
I will walk in the presence of the Lord
in the land of the living.   (From Psalm 116)

Gospel: Mark 8.27–35

By his multiplication of the loaves Jesus had demonstrated his creative power, but the crowd had not understood this; by restoring hearing and speech – a fulfilment of the prophecy of Isaiah – he had presented his credentials as the Messiah, but while the crowd seemed deeply impressed, they still thought of him as no more than a super prophet, as Peter reported when Jesus asked the Twelve who the people thought he was.

Jesus than asked the Twelve who they thought he was. Peter confidently affirmed that Jesus was the Christ, that is the Messiah. As Jesus had ordered the crowd not to spread abroad the news of his miracles, so now he ordered Peter not to publicize the fact that he was the Messiah. The reason for his command was that he knew the crowd were looking for a worldly Messiah, a mighty successor to the all-conquering King David. In today's Gospel we discover that the minds of Peter and the Twelve likewise were firmly confined within a worldly outlook. Peter simply refused to accept the fact that the Messiah would have to suffer and die. And so Jesus was constrained to rebuke him severely.

The perennial message of this incident is that we must be on our guard never to allow our religion to become a means of self-gratification. Faith is given us not in order that we may have power over others, nor even that we may be able to avoid suffering, but so that we may be able serve others, and give glory to God.

Sunday 25(B)

Old Testament thought:
If the virtuous man is God's son, God will help him
and rescue him from the clutches of his enemies.
Let us test him with cruelty and torture,
and thus explore this gentleness of his
and put his patience to the test.   (Wisdom 2.18–19)

Vocal prayer:
O God, save me by your name;
in your power, uphold my cause.
O God, hear my prayer;
listen to the words of my mouth.
For proud men have risen against me,
ruthless men seek my life.
They have no regard for God.
But I have God for my help.
The Lord upholds my life.
I will sacrifice to you with willing heart
and praise your name for it is good.

(From Psalm 54)

Gospel: Mark 9.30–37

The incident recorded in today's Gospel follows the Transfiguration, when Jesus revealed himself in glory, while speaking at the same time with two suffering figures of the Old Testament about his own imminent passing over in Jerusalem.

As they continue their journey through Galilee en route for Jerusalem, where Jesus will suffer and die, the Twelve react to his second prophecy of his passion, not with remonstration, but with mystified silence. They still cannot understand why the Messiah must suffer and die, nor do they see the connection between his passion and his glorification. It is this linking of divine glory with his suffering as man that is the great secret the disciples have hitherto been asked to keep. After this point in the Gospel Jesus never commands silence, because the secret is so soon to be revealed to all – when he declares to the High Priest who he is and what his glorious destiny is.

The continuing misunderstanding by the Twelve is shown now in their contending for places of honour in the Messianic kingdom. To demonstrate that the greatest must be the servant of all Jesus embraced a child, saying, 'Anyone who welcomes one of these little children in my name, welcomes me.' There is word-play in this saying, for in the Aramaic behind the Greek text the word for 'child' is also the word for 'servant'. The Twelve are thus being taught that they must welcome the status of servant and see the chief mark of discipleship, and of honour, in commitment to loving care of the weakest and neediest in the community.

Sunday 26(B)

Old Testament thought:
Moses answered: 'Are you jealous on my account? If only
the whole people of God were prophets!'

(Numbers 11.29)

Vocal prayer:
The law of the Lord is perfect,
it revives the soul.
The rule of the Lord is to be trusted,
it gives wisdom to the simple.
The fear of the Lord is holy
abiding for ever.
The decrees of the Lord are truth
and all of them just.

So in them your servant finds instruction;
great reward is in their keeping.
But who can detect his errors?
From hidden faults acquit me.   (From Psalm 19)

Gospel: Mark 9.38–43; 45; 47–48

The Gospel reading for today continues the theme of the Twelve's failure to grasp the true meaning of discipleship. They complain that someone who is not of their number is casting out devils in the Lord's name. This shows that they are jealous of their position and power, rather than happy to be able to do the Lord's work. The person who is casting out devils is doing so in Christ's name, which proves that he is a believer and also that he does not attribute power to himself but to Christ. This incident teaches us that the casting out of devils – which is a short-hand way of describing the fight against every kind of evil, especially moral evil, is the task of every believer, beginning with the evil in himself or herself.

In working for the kingdom of God none of us, not just those who are ordained, must never be jealous of others who also work for Christ. We are sometimes tempted to resent someone else doing a job that we normally do, especially if we do it well. We assert our position or status instead of being ready to submerge every impulse in the desire to see God's work done, whether by ourself or another; but humility requires also that no one should arrogate a competence he or she does not possess.

The rest of the passage urges us to take drastic measures to eradicate any weakness that might threaten our eternal salvation.

Sunday 27(B)

Old Testament thought:
The Lord God said, 'It is not good that the man should be
alone; I will make him a helpmate.'   (Genesis 2.18)

Vocal prayer:
O blessed are those who fear the Lord
and walk in his ways!
By the labour of your hands you shall eat;
you will be happy and prosper.
Your wife shall be like a fruitful vine
in the heart of your house;
your children like shoots of olive
around your table.
Indeed thus shall be blessed
the man who fears the Lord.
May the Lord bless you from Zion
in a happy Jerusalem
all the days of your life!
May you see your children's children.
On Israel, peace!   (Psalm 128)

Gospel: Mark 10.2–16

In today's Gospel we find Jesus perfecting the revelation given in the Old Testament. In speaking of marriage Jesus pointed back to a description of marriage as it was 'in the beginning', that is in the mind of God. Marriage has to be seen not as it may have become modified by this or that culture, but as it is and always has been according to God's design. The biblical description is given in pictorial or poetic language, for marriage is a mystery, a wonderful mixture of what is bodily with what is supernatural. The inspired writer tells us that the bond of marriage is so close that it is as if a wife is fashioned out of her husband's body (Genesis 2.18–25).

Because of this fact, Jesus stated categorically that the bond of true marriage can never be broken, and he rejected the legislation, found in Deuteronomy which allowed divorce – 'because of the hardness of your hearts'. The poetic description of the origin of marriage lies behind the early Christian writers' image of the Church, Christ's Bride, being born out of the pierced side of Christ on the Cross. The inspiration of scripture is seen here in that the Genesis story is a foreshadowing of the scene on the Cross.

Appended to these sayings of our Lord on marriage, Mark records a saying about children. In the society of that time a child had no rights. Mark is saying that no one has a right to enter the kingdom of God; we must enter through invitation and with the gratitude that a child shows on receiving a gift.

Sunday 28(B)

Old Testament thought:
I prayed, and understanding was given me;
I entreated, and the spirit of wisdom came to me.
I esteemed her more than sceptres and thrones;
compared with her, I held riches as nothing.

(Wisdom 7.7–8)

Vocal prayer:
God of our ancestors, Lord of mercy,
who by your word have made all things,
and by your wisdom have fitted man
to rule the creatures that have come from you,
to govern the world in holiness and justice
and in honesty of soul to wield authority,
grant me wisdom, the consort of your throne
and do not reject me from the number
of your children.   (Wisdom 9.1–4)

Gospel: Mark 10.17–30

The form of address: 'Good Teacher' was a fulsome compliment. A devout Jew was supposed to know that it was improper to call anyone 'good', and so Jesus rebuked the man. Moreover, the question: 'What must I do to inherit eternal life?' was insincere, and so Jesus brusquely pointed out, what the man ought already to have known, that keeping the Law was a requirement for entry into eternal life. The man claimed to have done this, but felt that something was lacking. Jesus knew well what that was. The man kept the Law but was unable to break his dependence upon worldly security, which for him, lay in his great wealth.

By looking at his disciples, Jesus indicated that all of them had to be on their guard against this weakness. It may not always be great wealth that is the problem, but we all find that there is something we are determined to hold onto at all costs, and it is this particular thing, to which we are so firmly attached, that constitutes the wealth that cannot get through the eye of a needle. It may seem that to attain such detachment is too difficult for us, but Jesus affirmed that the grace of God can enable us to find this virtue of detachment, without which even perfect keeping of the Law cannot guarantee entry into his kingdom.

Sunday 29(B)

Old Testament thought:
His soul's anguish over, he shall see the light and be
    content.
By his suffering shall my servant justify many,
taking their faults on himself.   (Isaiah 53.11)

Vocal prayer:
He has not despised
or disdained the poor man in his poverty,
has not hidden his face from him,
but has answered him when he called.

The whole earth will remember and come back to the
    Lord;
all families of nations will bow down before him.
And my soul will live for him, my children will serve him;
men will proclaim the Lord to generations yet to come,
his righteousness to a people yet unborn.
                                    (From Psalm 22)

Gospel: Mark 10.35–45

Against the background of Jesus' third prophecy of his Passion, James and John are discovered to be thinking only about their position in his kingdom. This trait had displayed itself earlier, but their attitude is all the more reprehensible now because they are beginning to glimpse the heavenly glory of that kingdom. They want places next to Jesus in heaven. Jesus does not deny them a place in glory, but points out that the disposition of things there belongs to the Father alone, and that to share in his glory means also to share in his baptism.

In the Old Testament baptism denoted being overwhelmed by calamity and suffering. James and John said that they were ready to accept this, but their enthusiasm reminds us of Peter's initial enthusiasm and later denial. The rest of the apostles, by their complaint over what James and John were asking, showed that they were just as bad. This episode gave Jesus an opportunity to speak to them about the meaning of authority and leadership in the Church. Leadership and authority are necessary in the Church, but the leader is in essence a servant, for Jesus had come not to be served but to serve. In the paragraph that precedes today's Gospel reading we are told that, 'They were on the road going up to Jerusalem; Jesus was walking ahead of them'. Leaders in the Church must follow him along that same road that led up to the city which housed the Temple of sacrifice.

Sunday 30(B)

Old Testament thought:
The deaf that day will hear the words of a book and, after
shadow and darkness the eyes of the blind will see.

(Isaiah 29.18)

Vocal prayer:
Now that daylight fills the sky,
We lift our hearts to God on high,
That he, in all we do or say,
Would keep us free from harm today.

Would guard our hearts and tongues from strife;
From anger's din would hide our life;
From all ill sights would turn our eyes;
Would close our ears from vanities.

Would keep our inmost conscience pure;
Our souls from folly would secure;
Would bid us check the pride of sense
With due and holy abstinence.

So we, when this new day is gone,
And night in turn is drawing on,
With conscience by the world unstained,
Shall praise his name for victory gained.

(Hymn from The Divine Office)

Gospel: Mark 10.46–52

One of the great biblical themes is the contrast between darkness and light, between blindness and sight; and for the Bible, physical blindness is a symbol of darkness of soul, lack of knowledge of God, of the absence of grace. We have been reading about the journey of Jesus and the Twelve towards Jerusalem, during which the Twelve evinced a dismal failure to understand the significance of the Passion, which Jesus repeatedly foretold. The journey was framed within two miracles of healing of blindness. On the first occasion Jesus commanded the healed man to say nothing about the miracle; he was not even to go into the village. At the end of the journey, however, the Twelve have begun, reluctantly, to face up to the fact that Jesus would suffer, and so Jesus no longer commanded silence, for it was now time for the Messianic secret to be revealed, and so the healed man was permitted to acclaim Jesus loudly as the Son of David, honouring Jesus with the royal Messianic title.

In the Greek idiom, to heal, and to save, are equivalent; Jesus gave the man not only physical sight but spiritual insight also; and the man's reaction was to follow Jesus – not merely in the physical sense, but by becoming a disciple – and he followed him along the road – which means along the road to Calvary. Our being healed of blindness requires that we too follow him along the same road.

Sunday 31(B)

Old Testament thought:
'Listen, Israel: The Lord your God is one Lord. You shall
love the Lord your God with all your heart, with all your
soul, and with all your strength.'

(Deuteronomy 6.4–6)

Vocal prayer:
I love you Lord, my strength,

my rock, my fortress, my saviour.

My God is the rock where I take refuge;

my shield, my mighty help, my stronghold.

My Lord is worthy of all praise;

when I call I am saved from my foes.

(From Psalm 18)

Gospel: Mark 12.28–34

Jesus had been asked a question by a scribe. The answers Jesus gave to his interrogators were shaped by his perception of their attitude. In this case Jesus warmed to the scribe, whom he recognized as a sincere questioner. He answered by quoting the Shema, which was recited every morning and evening by devout Jews. The word shema means 'listen'. The words that follow have been described as the Creed of Israel; but the very word is significant: the foundation of true piety is attention to the word of God.

The scribes discussed endlessly the relative importance of the multitude of precepts of the Law. Jesus told his questioner that the fundamental law was to love God without reservation. By stressing this law Jesus implied that all other law-keeping, all holiness, depends upon our relation with God himself.

Jesus then linked this basic law with the obligation to love our neighbour. He was the first to make this connection. He knew that love of neighbour flows necessarily from love of God; if we do not love our neighbour, that is proof that we do not love God. On the other hand we cannot love our neighbour unless we love God, for to love God is to open our minds to his truth, which alone teaches us what is good; and genuine love must be guided by knowledge of what is good.

Sunday 32(B)

Old Testament thought:
Elijah said: 'Please bring me a scrap of bread in your
hand'. The widow replied: 'I have only a handful of meal
and a little oil; I am going home to prepare this for myself
and my son to eat.' Elijah said: 'Do as you have said; but
first make a little scone for me.'

(From 1 Kings 17.10–16)

Vocal prayer:
It is the Lord who keeps faith for ever,
who is just to those who are oppressed.
It is he who gives bread to the hungry,
the Lord who sets prisoners free.
It is the Lord who gives sight to the blind,
who raises up those who are bowed down.
It is the Lord who loves the just,
the Lord who protects the stranger.
The Lord upholds the widow and orphan
but thwarts the path of the wicked.
The Lord will reign for ever,
Zion's God, from age to age.

(From Psalm 146)

Gospel: Mark 12.38–44

The incident recorded in today's Gospel contains Our Lord's last word on what it means to be a disciple. First Jesus denounced those scribes who made a show of religion and expected to be treated with deference, while at the same time they oppressed the poor. The widow, who put all she had into the offertory box, stands in marked contrast to such people and to all pseudo-religion. To point the importance of the scene Jesus called his disciples around him so that they would be sure to see what happened.

The widow put both of her coins into the box. She could so easily have put in one and kept the second for herself. Was she being imprudent and making herself a burden to others? Probably she lived from day to day and trusted that tomorrow she would find enough work to sustain her for that day, and so she gave everything she had left over. The lesson for us is that our Lord expects us to give all that we have to him, while at the same time learning how to be prudent and maintain ourselves and our families properly. But giving all has to do not just with material goods. Most of all, our Lord wants our company, as he wanted the company of Martha and Mary as he approached the hour of his death. That is why meditative prayer is so important. In our Lord's presence we find motivation and direction for all our actions.

The widow gave her all to the house of God: a day or two later Jesus gave his life. The story of the widow is thus a fitting ending to our Lord's teaching about discipleship.

Sunday 33(B)

Old Testament thought:
There is going to be a time of great distress, unparalleled
since the nations first came into existence. When that time
comes, your own people will be spared, all those whose
names are found written in the book.   (Daniel 12.1)

Vocal prayer:
O Lord, it is you who are my portion and cup;
it is you yourself who are my prize.
I keep the Lord ever in my sight:
since he is at my right hand and I shall stand firm.
And so my heart rejoices, my soul is glad;
even my body shall rest in safety.
For you will not leave my soul among the dead,
nor let your beloved know decay.
You will show me the path of life,
the fullness of joy in your presence,
at your right hand happiness for ever.

(From Psalm 16)

Gospel: Mark 13.24–32

Having finished asking and answering questions, and after pointing out to the Twelve the widow who gave her all to the Temple, as a perfect example of discipleship, Jesus spoke of the last or end things. The Greek word for 'end' is *eschaton* which gives us the English word 'eschatology', denoting the doctrine of the last things. Today's Gospel contains the eschatological discourse of Jesus.

Jesus adverted to the prophecy in Daniel which describes how, after a time of distress, at the end of time all of God's chosen ones, from the beginning of the world to its end, and whether alive or dead, will be gathered together into the brightness of God's eternal kingdom. As the structure of the cosmos and all physical forces within it begin to crumble, the Son of Man, that is our Lord Jesus Christ, will reveal himself in glory and usher in an unending era of peace and joy for the whole of redeemed Creation. In a parable, Jesus asserted that men and women are capable of reading the signs of nature; the believer ought similarly to be able to read the signs pertaining to supernatural happenings. The hint here is that Christians ought already to be observing the beginnings of this world's disintegration, and ought to be preparing for the Day of the Son of Man, that is the Day when Jesus will return to judge all mankind. At the same time Jesus stressed that no one, not even he, knows the date of his Second Coming. The signs tell us not the date of that event but that it might happen at any moment. We are now living in the end-time of the world's history. The end-time began on the day of the Resurrection and will continue until the Second Coming.

The above interpretation of the parable enables us to understand what Jesus meant when he said: 'Before this generation has passed away all these things will have taken place.' The great event which 'will have taken place' and which ushered in the end-time is the Paschal Mystery.

Our Lord's glorification on the Cross was also the beginning of the manifestation of his glory in his Bride, the Church. The Church is the embryo of his kingdom, and throughout the end-time his glory, though veiled, is seen by the eye of faith in the sacramental life of his Church.

Sunday 34(B): The Feast of Christ the Universal King

Old Testament thought:
I gazed into the visions of the night.
And I saw, coming on the clouds of heaven,
one like a son of man.
On him was conferred sovereignty, glory and kingship,
and men of all peoples, nations and languages
became his servants.
His sovereignty is an eternal sovereignty
which shall never pass away.   (Daniel 7.13–14)

Vocal prayer:
The Lord is king, with majesty enrobed;
the Lord had robed himself with might,
he has girded himself with power.
The world you made firm, not to be moved;
your throne has stood firm from of old.
From all eternity, O Lord, you are.
Truly your decrees are to be trusted;
holiness is fitting in your house,
O Lord, until the end of time.   (From Psalm 93)

Gospel: John 18:33–37

Pilate asked Jesus: 'What is truth?' There are countless truths that are useful to know, but by 'truth' Jesus meant more than the sum of human knowledge. He had come, he told Pilate, so that men and women might know the truth; but knowledge, in the biblical sense, embraced the notion of union with that which one knows – like the knowledge husband and wife have of each other, and so, to know the truth, in this sense, means to become united with God, who is the source of all truth.

By dying on the Cross and being raised from the dead, Jesus gained for us a share in God's Spirit, in his life. By sharing in the life of God in this way we are enabled to live according to the truth. The world is divided into those who live according to their own truths, and those who 'are on the side of Truth', that is those who seek to be ruled entirely by the Spirit of God. The latter group know that the truth has to be revealed to them by God, and so they listen to the voice of Christ, through prayer and attention to the teaching of those whom Christ appointed to speak in his name; and thus they become instruments in the extension of the kingdom of God upon earth. This kingdom does not emerge from below, like the beasts Daniel saw coming up out of the sea, but comes down from heaven, as Daniel saw the Son of Man coming on clouds of glory.

Sundays in Ordinary Time, Cycle C

Sunday 13(C)

Old Testament thought:
Elisha turned away, took the pair of oxen and slaughtered them. He used the plough for cooking the oxen, then gave to his men, who ate. He then rose and followed Elijah and became his servant. (1 Kings 19.21)

Vocal prayer:
Preserve me, God, I take refuge in you.
I say to the Lord: 'You are my God'.
O Lord, it is you who are my portion and cup;
it is you yourself who are my prize.
I will bless the Lord who gives me counsel,
who even at night directs my heart.
I keep the Lord ever in my sight,
since he is at my right hand, I shall stand firm.
And so my heart rejoices, my soul is glad;
even my body shall rest in safety.
For you will not leave my soul among the dead,
nor let your beloved know decay. (From Psalm 16)

Gospel: Luke 9.51–62

On Mount Tabor Jesus had granted his three closest disciples a vision of him speaking to Moses and Elijah about his 'passing', to be accomplished in Jerusalem. The vision had also presented him in transfigured form – a previewing of his resurrection glory. Mount Tabor was the watershed in Jesus' ministry: he now left Galilee and set his face resolutely to go to Jerusalem where he would offer himself in sacrifice.

On their journey towards Jerusalem Jesus rebuked the disciples for desiring to punish the inhospitable Samaritans by calling down fire from heaven to burn them up. This desire was a sign that they still thought of the Messiah as a conqueror in the worldly sense. But his kingdom was to be established through meekness and love. Luke records in the Acts of the Apostles how not long after the Lord's resurrection the Samaritans heard and accepted the Gospel.

Further along the road to Jerusalem, they met a would-be disciple. The encounter provided Jesus with an opportunity to speak of the total commitment that is demanded of every disciple. Jesus never denied that there are many serious obligations in life which his disciples should honour, but he insisted that anything required of a disciple for the sake of the kingdom of God takes priority over every other obligation.

Sunday 14(C)

Old Testament thought:
Like a son comforted by his mother will I comfort you.
And by Jerusalem you will be comforted.   (Isaiah 66.13)

Vocal prayer:
Cry out with joy to God all the earth,
O sing to the glory of his name;
O render him glorious praise.
Say to God: 'How tremendous your deeds!'
Come and hear, all you who fear God.
I will tell what he did for my soul.
Blessed be God who did not reject my prayer,
nor withhold his love from me.   (From Psalm 66)

Gospel: Luke 10.1–12; 17–20

Jesus sent out messengers to prepare people in places he would himself visit. Our Lord had in mind – and Luke was aware of this – not primarily places on the route between Galilee and Jerusalem, upon which he was then travelling, but the whole world which he would visit at the end of time on the Day of Judgement. And so this incident is prophetic of the worldwide and continuous mission of the Church after our Lord's ascension.

Relevant to this fact is also the choosing of seventy messengers. This indicates the enormous future expansion of the Church when twelve apostles will no longer be sufficient to perform the work of evangelization. The powers with which our Lord endowed these seventy, who foreshadowed the future pastors of the Church, were the same as the powers he gave to the Twelve. Moreover the number seventy, corresponding to the number of nations listed in Genesis 10 hints at the worldwide context of the mission of the seventy, and it happens also to be the number of elders that Moses selected to ease the burden of his work when the people were too many for him to handle alone.

Note that the first word the messengers of Christ are commanded to speak when they enter a house is 'Peace' – our Lord's first word to his disciples on the first Easter day. The peace that our Lord offers is, however, no lazy comfortable idleness but the peace that arises from reconciliation of men and women with God, through forgiveness, and with each other, likewise through mutual forgiveness. Thus our Lord followed his blessing of peace (John 20.20–23) with the promise of reconciliation through their ministry of reconciliation.

Sunday 15(C)

Old Testament thought:
The word is very near you;
it is in your mouth and in your heart
for your observance.   (Deuteronomy 30.14)

Vocal prayer:
Happy the man who considers the poor and the weak.
The Lord will save him in the day of evil,
will guard him, give him life, make him happy in the land
and will not give him up to the will of his foes.
The Lord will help him on his bed of pain,
he will bring him back from sickness to health.
As for me, I said. 'Lord, have mercy on me,
heal my soul for I have sinned against you'.
My foes are speaking evil against me.
'How long before he dies and his name be forgotten?'
They come to visit me and speak empty words,
their hearts full of malice, they spread it abroad.

(From Psalm 41)

Gospel: Luke 10.25–37

Still on their journey to Jerusalem but now in Jewish
territory, Jesus and his disciples met a lawyer who tried to
embarrass them by asking: 'What must I do to inherit
eternal life?' As if saying: 'You don't really have a problem
– you know the answer very well', Jesus made the lawyer
answer the question himself, which he did by quoting
Deuteronomy 6.5.

The fundamental law of God is not some hidden puzzle,
for it is written in our hearts. His commandment is that
we love him and our neighbour unreservedly. If there is
a problem it lies in ourselves, in our stifling the voice of
conscience which speaks to us in this law.

A little crestfallen, the lawyer tried to justify his question
by asking: 'But how do I identify my neighbour?' Again
Jesus led him on to find the answer for himself. He did
this by telling the parable of the Good Samaritan. No
doubt the parable contains several lessons, but its purpose
is not to provoke self-righteous indignation at the hard-
heartedness of the priest and the Levite who saw the
injured man but left him lying at the roadside. Their
motive was probably not insensitivity but their fear of
becoming ritually unclean through contact with a corpse,
and so be disqualified from performing their duties in the
Temple to which they were on their way.

Whatever the motives of the priest and the Levite who
left the man lying there, our Lord constructed the parable
so as to shift the emphasis of the question from, 'Should
the two have regarded the half-dead man as their neighbour?' to, 'Which of the passers-by was neighbour to the
victim?' Anyone who needs care and love – and who
doesn't? – is my neighbour; but am I his neighbour?

Sunday 16(C)

Old Testament thought:
Then taking cream, milk and the calf he had prepared, he
laid it all before them, and they ate while he remained
standing near them under the tree.   (Genesis 18.8)

Vocal prayer:
The Lord is my light and my salvation;
whom need I fear?
The Lord is the fortress of my life;
of whom should I be afraid?
One thing I ask of the Lord,
one thing I seek:
to live in the house of the Lord
all the days of my life,
to enjoy the sweetness of the Lord
and to consult him in his Temple.
My heart has said of you,
'seek his face'.
Lord, I do seek your face;
do not hide your face from me.   (From Psalm 27)

Gospel: Luke 10.38–42

If we feel that our Lord was unfair to Martha, that is because we make the same mistake as she did. Jesus approved her work but not her state of mind. She was 'anxious and troubled', distracted by what she was doing. Mary, on the other hand perceived what was the one thing that mattered: that she, and her sister, should seize the opportunity of listening to Jesus. The incarnate Word was in their home; what did his bodily needs count beside his desire to bless them with his word. Mary, by her act of keen listening, was worshipping him. She knew that he had come amongst us not to be served but to serve, and she gave him an opportunity to do this.

Jesus is the Word of God; our first duty is to listen to him. True, he may ask us to serve him, but even our legitimate service must never blind us to the fact that seeking his presence and attending to his word is the homage that pleases him most. In Acts 6.1–6 we find a sequel to today's Gospel incident. The apostles found themselves becoming preoccupied with works of corporal mercy and so they extended the leadership structure of the Church to include deacons, so that the specific work of the apostles, viz. prayer and the ministry of the word, would not be impeded, while at the same time the corporal works of mercy would not be neglected.

Sunday 17(C)

Old Testament thought:
On the day I called, you answered me, O Lord.

(From Psalm 138)

Vocal prayer:
I thank you, Lord, with all my heart;
you have heard the words of my mouth.
Before all the angels I will bless you;
I will adore before your temple.
I thank you for your faithfulness and love
which excel all we ever knew of you.
On the day I called, you answered;
you increased the strength of my soul.
You stretch out your hand and save me,
your hand will do all things for me.
Your love, O Lord, is eternal,
discard not the work of your hands.

(From Psalm 138)

Gospel: Luke 11.1–13

The apostles wanted to find that union with almighty God which Jesus enjoyed when he prayed, and so they asked him to teach them to pray. The prayer he taught them is a model for prayer and also an implicit statement of Christian faith.

Jesus, the eternal Son made flesh, prayed to God the Father: the Christian must do likewise. Although offered through the Son, in the power of the Spirit, prayer is directed to the Father, and begins with adoration: 'Father, may your name be held holy, your kingdom come'. Prayer's foundation, in any of its modes, is preoccupied with the majesty, wisdom, and love of God. We pray initially not for what we want but for what he desires.

Then we place our needs before him. Observe it is *our* needs. He is *our* Father and we ask for our daily bread – food for body and soul. Prayer is still turned outwards from the individual, and this petition implies that the kingdom of God has very much to do with the unity of mankind.

The next thought is of forgiveness – the forgiveness we all seek from the Father and, linked with that, forgiveness between individuals, which is the cement of our unity. The concluding petition is an act of humility, acknowledging our need of the Father's protection against the powers of darkness.

In two parables which follow the prayer Jesus emphasizes the need for perseverance in prayer. Perseverance rests on the unshakeable belief that God the Father is love itself and will never be less loving than a sinful earthly father.

Observe the note on which the parables end. The great gift we receive is the Holy Spirit, who creates that union with God the Father which our Lord enjoyed when he prayed.

Sunday 18(C)

Old Testament thought:
What does he gain for all the toil and strain he has under-
gone under the sun?   (Ecclesiastes 2.22)

Vocal prayer:
   O that today you would listen to his voice!
   Harden not your hearts.
Come, ring our joy to the Lord;
hail the rock who saves us!
Let us come before him giving thanks;
with songs let us hail the Lord.
   O that today you would listen to his voice!
   Harden not your hearts.
Come in; let us bow and bend low;
let us kneel before the God who made us
for he is our God and we
the flock that is led by his hand.
   O that today you would listen to his voice!
   Harden not your hearts.   (From Psalm 95)

Gospel: Luke 12.13–21

In the Parable of the Rich Fool Jesus does not answer the question he has been asked, for the questioner is too deeply engrossed in worldly concerns to deserve an answer. In the parable Jesus does not condemn industry that is inspired by a responsible attitude to our worldly needs, but only the mentality that sees no end beyond the amassing of wealth, in the belief that such wealth will provide perfect security. Anyone who thinks in that way has become the slave of his possessions and is a fool. In practice such a man has become an atheist, for he has stifled the knowledge that he is a son of God whom God loves and for whom God has prepared an eternal inheritance.

The wise man, in contrast, lives in the light of this knowledge, seeking to earn virtue by loving God and his neighbour, thus directing his industry towards true riches and towards material things only in so far as they help him towards that end.

Sunday 19(C)

Old Testament thought:
This was the expectation of your people, the saving of the
virtuous and the ruin of their enemies.

(Wisdom 18.7)

Vocal prayer:
Shout with joy to the Lord, all virtuous men,
praise comes well from upright hearts;
happy the nation whose God is the Lord,
the people he has chosen for his heritage.
See how the eye of the Lord is on those who fear him,
on those who rely on his love,
to rescue their souls from death,
and keep them alive in famine.

Our soul awaits the Lord;
he is our help and shield.
Our hearts rejoice in him,
we trust in his holy name.
Lord, let your love rest on us
as our hope has rested in you.   (From Psalm 33)

Gospel: Luke 12.32–48

Developing the teaching of last Sunday's parable, today's Gospel reading urges all believers to seek heavenly treasure. Detachment from worldly possessions and pleasures is presented not as suffering misery but as joyful expectation of the life of God's kingdom. Those who sell their possessions and give to the poor are motivated by trust in God's goodness.

Christian wakefulness in expectation of our Lord's return was prefigured by the Passover-vigil of the Israelites on the night they were delivered from Egypt. The faithful in any age can become discouraged and even lose faith on account of their being so few in number, compared with the rest of mankind. The Israelites were relatively few, but they were delivered. And so Jesus said to his disciples: 'There is no need for you to be afraid, little flock, for it has pleased your Father to give you the kingdom.'

Our Lord then addressed the subject of the special preparedness that must be found amongst those to whom much has been given, that is to the stewards of his mysteries, the apostles and their successors. Although the warning given here is addressed particularly to the ordained servants of the Lord, it applies to all disciples, for each one in his own way has received much, in the sense that he is given a specific task that no other person can perform. In his own sphere all depends on him. All must be found awake, performing their allotted tasks on that day when the Lord returns to establish his kingdom for ever.

Sunday 20(C)

Old Testament thought:
'Let this man be put to death.' So they took Jeremiah and
threw him into the well. There was no water in the well,
only mud, and into the mud Jeremiah sank.

(From Jeremiah 38.4–6)

Vocal prayer:
I waited and waited for the Lord;
now at last he stooped to me
and heard my cry for help.
He has pulled me out of the horrible pit,
out of the slough of the marsh,
has settled my feet on a rock
and steadied my steps.
He has put a new song in my mouth,
a song of praise to our God;
dread will seize many at the sight,
and they will put their trust in the Lord.
To me, poor wretch,
come quickly, Lord!
my helper, my saviour, my God,
come and do not delay!

(From Psalm 40)

Gospel: Luke 12.49–53

'Fire' in biblical usage speaks of the judgement of God. As he drew near to Jerusalem Jesus became overwhelmed by the knowledge that a great judgement was about to take place; he trembled at the thought, for he knew that it was he who would suffer in this judgement. When he spoke of the baptism he was about to endure, the word 'baptism' was equivalent to 'fire'. Just as Jeremiah had been lowered down into a slimy pit, so Jesus would descend into the realms of suffering and death.

'Fire' and 'water' conjure up other images besides those of divine judgement; they speak also of cleansing, of purification, and point to the Holy Spirit by whose power such purification is effected. Obediently submitting to the judgement of God, Jesus would overthrow the power of evil and lead mankind into a new life of holiness and joy.

In conclusion, in this short discourse, Jesus returns to the concept of judgement. He will become a sign that separates men and women into two camps: those who love and obey him and those who resist his grace and defy him. By reacting to Jesus in these two opposite ways men and women become divided amongst themselves. Our Lord did not desire that this be so, but it is bound to happen because men and women are free to choose him or to reject him. Jesus offers salvation to all but he cannot force the unwilling to accept it.

Sunday 21(C)

Old Testament thought:
Now towards her I send flowing peace, like a river, and
like a stream in spate the glory of the nations.

(Isaiah 66.12)

Vocal prayer:
   Go out to the whole world;
   proclaim the Good News.
O praise the Lord, all you nations,
acclaim him all you peoples!
Strong is his love for us;
he is faithful for ever.
   Go out to the whole world,
   proclaim the Good News.

(Psalm 117)

Gospel: Luke 13.22–30

Jesus did not really answer the question about the number of souls who will be saved. Only God the Father knows that number, and such knowledge cannot be given to human beings. What men and women need to know is that they could be excluded from the kingdom of God. The parable tells us that when they come knocking on the door, the master of the house may say that he does not even know them.

What was the defect in those who were excluded? It was presumption. They presumed that because they had associated with the Jesus in the streets and even at table, they were bound to be welcomed by him into his eternal home. By this parable Jesus unmasked the superficiality of such companionship. They heard his teaching, but had they acted upon it? The parable was directed first of all against the closed-minded amongst the religious establishment who heard Jesus teaching but shut their hearts against him, while relying for their salvation upon their descent from Abraham. Jesus affirmed – as Isaiah had done before – that the kingdom would be opened to all of mankind, and many pagans might well enter the kingdom sooner and with greater ease than those who were originally chosen. Sad to say this very fact can and does give rise to a new kind of presumption: 'The kingdom is for all – I've got a free pass – no need to worry'.

Sunday 22(C)

Old Testament thought:
The greater you are, the more humbly you should
behave, and then you will find favour with the Lord; for
great though the power of the Lord is, he accepts the
homage of the humble. There is no cure for the proud
man's malady.

(Ecclesiasticus 3.18–20; 28)

Vocal prayer:
The just shall rejoice in the presence of God,
shall exult and dance for joy.
O sing to the Lord, make music to his name;
rejoice in the Lord, exult in his presence.
Father of the orphan, defender of the widow,
such is God in his holy place.
God gives the lonely a place to live in;
he leads the prisoners forth into freedom.

(From Psalm 68)

Gospel: Luke 14.1; 7–14

'There is no cure for the proud man's malady' (Ecclesiasticus 3.28). Jesus taught that with God all things are possible. We believe therefore that there can be a cure even for this malady. Nonetheless in spite of God's help pride is very difficult to eradicate for, in different ways, pride exerts an insidious influence upon everyone.

The incident recorded in today's Gospel describes how on social occasions people like to be seen in a prominent place. This bolsters their self-esteem. In his parable Jesus seems to appeal to self-interest, saying that if one at first takes a humble place there is a chance that one will be honoured by the host's invitation to go up higher. Jesus does not condemn absolutely the desire in men and women to be rewarded, but they must realize that it is the host who has the right to reward us. By submitting to this we show humility.

Most important in this parable is the exposing of the ulterior motives of the host who asks people to his table in order to further his own interests. His pride is closely allied to greed and desire for power. This form of pride is much more abhorrent to God than the more childish desire of the guests to gain approval. True hospitality would have been shown had he invited the needy. In this parable Jesus is not forbidding us to entertain our friends and relations, but to avoid doing so in the hope of receiving something in return. At the Last Supper Jesus, the perfect host, washed the disciples' feet.

Sunday 23(C)

Old Testament thought:
As for your intention, who could have learnt it had you
not granted wisdom and sent your Holy Spirit from
above?   (Wisdom 9.17)

Vocal prayer:
To your eyes a thousand years
are like yesterday, come and gone,
no more than a watch in the night.
Make us know the shortness of our life
that we may gain wisdom of heart.
Lord, relent! Is your anger for ever?
Show pity on your servants.
In the morning fill us with your love;
we shall rejoice and exult all our days,
Let the favour of the Lord be upon us:
give success to the work of our hands.

(From Psalm 90)

Gospel: Luke 14.25–33

As Jesus came closer to Jerusalem, the place of sacrifice, he was beginning to attract great crowds. He knew how shallow a crowd's enthusiasm can be and so told them how demanding following him could be. His disciples must love no one so much that they put that person before serving him. That is the meaning behind the Hebrew verb 'to hate'.

Then he told two parables which counselled would-be disciples to weigh up carefully what discipleship might mean. Not all disciples would be assigned the same task nor would all be required to show the same degree of detachment from natural responsibilities; but this does not mean that one form of service of Christ is superior to another. The quality of discipleship, the holiness of the disciple, depends not upon the seeming importance of the task given but solely on the perfection of his carrying out his task; but from all is demanded total detachment from whatever might tempt them to put the work of the kingdom in second place.

Underlying the whole scene is the thought that a disciple must obtain the wisdom to enable him to assess his own capacity for the task he proposes to take up. Having gained sufficient self-knowledge to do this he then realizes that he will be required to persevere to the end, and that the end could be a cross.

The wisdom to obtain this sort of disposition of mind and heart is a gift from God, who is Wisdom itself, and can be obtained only through humble prayer.

Sunday 24(C)

Old Testament thought:
The Lord says this: 'Am I likely to take pleasure in the
death of a wicked man and not prefer to see him
renounce his wickedness and live?'   (Ezekiel 18.23)

Vocal prayer:
Have mercy on me, O God, in your goodness;
in your tenderness wipe away my faults,
wash me clean of my guilt,
purify me from my sin.
For I am well aware of my faults,
I have my sin constantly in mind.
Having sinned against none other than you,
having done what you regard as wrong.
Instil some joy and gladness into me,
let the bones you have crushed rejoice again.
Hide your face from my sins,
wipe out all my guilt.
God, create a clean heart in me,
put in me a new and constant spirit.
Do not banish me from your presence,
do not deprive me of your holy spirit.

(From Psalm 51)

Gospel: Luke 15.1–32

There are three parables in the Gospel reading for this Sunday; in each something precious has been lost and then found. The most striking and developed parable is that in which a son is morally lost and then found. Because of our preoccupation with this lost and more colourful son, we are tempted to overlook that which makes sense of the story: the intense love the father has for his son.

Day after day the old man walked out to the boundary of his estate, straining his eyes to catch sight of his returning son – for he never gave him up as lost for ever. When at last the prodigal son appeared, the father ran out to meet him and embraced him. It is the father who is prodigal – absurdly prodigal with his mercy and love.

A second point that is often overlooked is that this is a parable about two sons. The behaviour of the elder son merits closer attention. Jesus wanted to depict clearly the contrast between two sorts of people whom he met as he travelled around the country. On the one side there were the dissolute – the prostitutes and the swindlers, on the other side were the self-nominated righteous – many of them scribes and Pharisees. The former group did not claim any right to enter God's kingdom, but they were capable of repentance and would accept forgiveness were it offered them; the second group however resented the idea that they needed forgiveness, believing that by their righteousness they had a claim on membership of God's kingdom.

The concluding message of the parable is that none of us can demand a place at the heavenly feast as of right. Seats at our Lord's heavenly banquet are by invitation only; but he invites us all.

Sunday 25(C)

Old Testament thought:
Seek good and not evil so that you may live.
Hate evil, love good, maintain justice at the city gate.

(Amos 5.14–15)

Vocal prayer:
You servants of the Lord, praise,
praise the name of the Lord!
Blessed be the name of the Lord,
henceforth and for ever!
From east to west,
praised be the name of the Lord!
He raises the poor from the dust;
he lifts the needy from the dunghill
to give them a place with princes,
with the princes of his people.
He enthrones the barren woman in her house
by making her the happy mother of sons.

(From Psalm 113)

Gospel: Luke 16.1–13

The parable of the crooked estate steward troubles many people, for they mistakenly think that our Lord is commending him for his swindling. The prophet Amos makes it quite clear that true religion abhors all such wickedness, and our Lord condemns it even more strongly.

In his parable our Lord chose this con man in order to capture his hearers' attention; then he commended the man not for his crookedness but for his thoroughness and industry. The man worked very hard to ensure that when he was dismissed from office he would not starve.

Such people, our Lord said, are wiser in their own way than the children of light, that is Christian believers, who in contrast with the wicked steward are far too lazy in attending to their spiritual welfare. Those who believe the gospel and hope for eternal life ought to expend the utmost energy in making sure that they will have friends who by their prayers will help them reach the heavenly mansions, and welcome when they get there. These friends are the people to whom they showed charity in this life. This parable is above all an exhortation to give alms.

When we are tempted to disparage people whom we think are too interested in getting on in this world, we should ask ourselves if we are energetic enough in our attempts to advance in the spiritual world. The stakes there are much higher.

Sunday 26(C)

Old Testament thought:
Woe to those esconced so snugly in Zion and to those who
feel so safe on the mountains of Samaria.   (Amos 6.1)

Vocal prayer:
The law of the Lord is perfect,
it revives the soul.
The rule of the Lord is to be trusted,
it gives wisdom to the simple.
The fear of the Lord is holy,
abiding for ever.
The decrees of the Lord are truth
and all of them just.
So in them your servant finds instruction;
great reward is in their keeping.
But who can detect all his errors?
From hidden faults acquit me.   (From Psalm 19)

Gospel: Luke 16.19–31

Once again we are prepared for the Gospel reading by a denunciation by Amos against those who are living in luxury. Our Lord's parable is about a rich man who within his mansion dines and wines voluptuously, while on his doorsteps a poor man starves and is comforted only by dogs licking his sores.

By the end of the Old Testament period the Jews had come to believe that in this life injustice may remain, and wickedness seem to triumph. But because of their unshakeable belief in God's justice and love, they had reached the notion that there must be a life beyond this one when justice will be done. Our Lord's parable follows this tradition. In heaven the tables are turned; the beggar finds comfort, the rich man pain.

Then come affirmations of fundamental truths. At death a person's destiny is fixed. He is either on the way up or on the way down, and there is no crossing over from either side to the other. In desperation the rich man suggests that his brothers might be persuaded to mend their ways if they were warned by someone who had risen from the dead. No, they are told: they already have knowledge of the law – they have consciences – and only those who try to obey their conscience will be able to accept a message from one risen from the dead.

In this parable our Lord alludes to his own resurrection, and teaches that a prerequisite for receiving the gift of faith in his resurrection is the desire to obey God's law. The law, as St Paul explained, is a schoolmaster who leads us to Christ, to faith in Christ and in his resurrection.

Sunday 27(C)

Old Testament thought:
For the fig tree is not going to blossom,
nor will there be any fruit on the vine,
the yield of the olive will fail,
the fields afford no food;
the sheep will vanish from the fold,
nor will there be any cattle in the stalls.
But I will rejoice in the Lord,
I will exult in God my saviour.   (Habakkuk 3.17–18)

Vocal prayer:
Come, ring out our joy to the Lord;
hail the rock who saves us.
Let us come before him, giving thanks,
with songs let us praise the Lord.
Come in, let us bow and bend low;
let us kneel before the God who made us
for he is our God and we
the people who belong to his pasture,
the flock that is led by his hand.
O that today you would listen to his voice!
Harden not your hearts as at Meribah,
as on that day at Massah in the desert
when your fathers put me to the test;
when they tried me, though they saw my works.

(From Psalm 95)

Gospel: Luke 17.1–10

The prophet Habakkuk exhorted the people to remain true to the Lord in spite of their suffering. They had to learn that faith is not just believing in God but also remaining faithful to him whatever the circumstances. What was it that troubled the apostles and moved them to ask our Lord to increase their faith? The clue is given in verses 3 and 4. It was not primarily oppression from outside but the burden of fulfilling his commandments, in particular that of forgiving those who wronged them over and over again. Jesus tells the apostles that if they have even a grain of true faith, that is trust in him and obedience to his commandments, they will be able to overcome this mountainous difficulty. He is not suggesting that they try to prove their faith by transplanting forests into the sea.

Along with the metaphor of moving trees he uses that of the servant who, coming home from a hard day's work, serves his master before sitting down to his own supper, for this is what he has contracted to do. So with the disciple he is contracted to serve his master, and ought not to think that by obeying the master's command he is doing anything extraordinary that deserves special reward.

In forgiving graciously and without stint we are not being heroes but simply obeying his command and so being given the privilege of becoming like him.

Sunday 28(C)

Old Testament thought:
'Your servant will no longer offer sacrifice to any god
except the Lord.'   (2 Kings 5.17)

Vocal prayer:
Sing a new song to the Lord
for he has worked wonders.
His right hand and his holy arm
have brought salvation.
The Lord has made known his salvation;
has shown his justice to the nations.
He has remembered his truth and love
for the house of Israel.
All the ends of the earth have seen
the salvation of our God.
Shout to the Lord of all the earth,
ring out your joy.   (From Psalm 98)

Gospel: Luke 17.11–19

For the Jew of our Lord's day disease seemed to have a connection with sin. Some of them still thought that it was a punishment for actual sin. Our Lord refuted this notion, but when he healed people he wanted them to see beyond physical healing to the healing of their souls through his forgiveness.

Disease is one of the manifestations of the disorder that afflicts mankind as a result of the Fall, and leprosy is a fitting symbol of this fact on account of the way it permeates the whole body. And so the healing of the ten lepers was a sign that Jesus had overcome the power of Satan and liberated mankind from enslavement to sin.

An important feature of the story of the ten lepers is their reaction. Only one came back to give thanks, and he was a foreigner, like Naaman of old who had been so grateful for his healing that he asked to be allowed to take home some earth from the land of Israel so that he could worship the God of that land.

This Gospel incident ends therefore in the implicit indictment of those who think that their membership of the chosen people entitles them to divine favours for which they need not even give thanks.

The gratitude of the Samaritan declared not merely his joy at receiving physical health but also his appreciation of having been accepted by God. He was no longer a foreigner, alienated from the kingdom of God.

Sunday 29(C)

Old Testament thought:
As long as Moses kept his arms raised, Israel had the
advantage; when he let his arms fall, the advantage went
to Amalek.   (Exodus 17.11)

Vocal prayer:
I lift up my eyes to the mountains;
from where shall come my help?
My help shall come from the Lord
who made heaven and earth.
May he never allow you to stumble!
Let him sleep not, your guard.
No, he sleeps not nor slumbers,
Israel's guard.
The Lord will guard you from evil,
he will guard your soul.
The Lord will guard your going and coming
both now and for ever.   (From Psalm 121)

Gospel: Luke 18.1–8

On their journey towards the Promised Land, where they were destined to institute true worship of the one true God, and to be moulded into a people whose stock would provide a human nature for the Messiah, the Israelites encountered many obstacles, not least confrontation with the powerful Amalekites. The most serious sin the people of God could commit was to lose heart and mistrust the power of God.

The book of Exodus tells us how Moses persevered in prayer all day long as the battle raged. Victory came to the Israelites not through their own strength but through God's providence and the prayer of Moses. The image of Moses with uplifted hands – the posture adopted still today by the priest when celebrating the eucharist – helps our meditation on prayer. Our Lord's parable tells the same story. With a touch of humour our Lord describes how a reluctant judge is compelled to give a favourable judgement simply because the plaintiff pesters him mercilessly.

On our life's journey towards the Promised Land we encounter enormous obstacles. Our Lord urges us to persevere. Today's Gospel develops and underlines the message of the Gospel of two weeks ago. Persevering prayer is the expression of the faith that remains firm in the face of apparent defeat. We have to sustain this kind of faith to the very end. 'When the Son of Man comes will he find any faith on the earth?'

Sunday 30(C)

Old Testament thought:
The humble man's prayer pierces the clouds.

(Ecclesasticus 35.17)

Vocal prayer:
I will bless the Lord at all times;
his praise always on my lips.
In the Lord my soul will make its boast;
the humble will hear and be glad.
The Lord turns his face against the wicked
to destroy their remembrance from the earth.
The just call, and the Lord hears
and rescues them in all their distress.
The Lord is close to the broken-hearted;
those whose spirit is crushed he will save.
The Lord ransoms the souls of his servants.
Those who hide in him shall not be condemned.

(From Psalm 34)

Gospel: Luke 18.9–14

The parable of the Pharisee and the sinful tax-collector re-introduces the teaching of the Parable of the Two Sons. The Pharisee was proud of his moral performance, and he presented it to God as a demand to be admitted into God's presence. The sinful tax-collector, on the other hand, had nothing to be proud of, and so threw himself upon God's mercy. By this very act he acknowledged that God is love, and in so doing had already turned to God in adoration. He was turned towards God, the Pharisee towards himself.

By thinking that his creditable moral score gave him a claim upon God, the Pharisee betrayed blindness to the enormous demand that God's law makes upon men and women – perfect love of God and of our neighbour. In face of this demand all must acknowledge that their acceptance into the heavenly kingdom depends entirely upon God's grace.

It is true that we are required to make every effort to observe the commandments and even the lesser precepts that help us on our way towards perfection; but while religious and moral practice is important, it is not the heart of the matter. The heart of the matter is the humility which prompts us to pray: 'A pure heart create in me, O Lord, and renew a right spirit within me.'

Sunday 31(C)

Old Testament thought:
You spare all things because all things are yours, Lord,
lover of life.   (Wisdom 11.27)

Vocal prayer:
I will give you glory, O God my King.
I will bless your name for ever.
I will bless you day after day
and praise your name for ever.
The Lord is kind and full of compassion,
slow to anger, abounding in love.
How good is the Lord to all,
compassionate to all his creatures.
The Lord is faithful in all his words,
and loving in all his deeds.
The Lord supports all who fall
and raises all who are bowed down.   (From Psalm 145)

Gospel: Luke 19.1–10

Jesus has just restored sight to a blind man, and the crowd were following him, full of excitement and joy, giving praise to God. Zacchaeus, a rich tax-collector, was among the crowd; he wanted very much to see Jesus, but he was so small that he had to climb up a sycamore tree to get a glimpse of him. Zacchaeus may well have been suffering pangs of conscience, on account of the shady way in which he had been making money, but the tradition of his people encouraged him to trust in God's mercy, for the God of Israel was 'a lover of life' who even when he punished did so gently, for he desired not the death of the sinner but that he would repent and live. The little story about Zacchaeus complements the parable we read last week by filling out the concept of repentance. First, the penitent is moved by grace to trust our Lord and to want to see him; our Lord responds immediately to this desire by making known his desire to meet the penitent; not only does he want to meet him but wants to come and visit him in his home – to share life with him. 'Zacchaeus, come down. Hurry, because I must stay at your house today.' Our Lord's forgiveness is no mere amnesty for past misdeeds but the offer of real friendship. He tells us that he likes us. Finally Zacchaeus offers gladly to make reparation for his past misdeeds.

The incident concerning Zacchaeus provides a model for us of the way we should approach and celebrate the sacrament of reconciliation.

Sunday 32(C)

Old Testament thought:
The King of the world will raise us up, since it is for his laws that we die, to live again for ever.

(2 Maccabees 7.9)

Vocal prayer:
Lord, hear a cause that is just;

pay heed to my cry.

Turn your ear to my prayer: no deceit is on my lips.

I kept my feet firmly on your paths;

there was no faltering in my steps.

I am here and I call, you will hear me, O God.

Hide me in the shadow of your wings.

As for me, I shall see your face,

and be filled, when I awake, with the sight of your glory.

(From Psalm 17)

Gospel: Luke 20.27; 34–38

Close to the hour of his death, Jesus encountered some Sadducees, men belonging to the priestly caste and the aristocratic laity. These denied the resurrection, appealing to the five books of Moses which do not mention a resurrection.

In early times the Israelites thought of immortality as family continuity, hence the concern about offspring. The Law required that if a man died childless, his brother had a duty to marry the widow in the hope that she would have children and so confer a kind of immortality upon his brother.

This is the background to the encounter with the Sadducees who tried to make Jesus look foolish by asking which of seven brothers, to all of whom a woman had been married according to this law, would be her husband in the resurrection-life. Jesus in his turn upbraided them for their perverse blindness to spiritual reality. The Sadducees thought of the resurrection-life as no more than a continuation of this life. They had no sense of the mystery of God and of life. In the life to come, he told them, there is no need for procreation which is a basic function of marriage in earth, for in the resurrection there is no coming into being and no dying.

Finally Jesus confounded them by quoting the books of Scripture they had relied on. That there is a state of eternal being is implicit in the revelation to Moses at the burning bush. God said: 'I am the God of Abraham, of Isaac, and of Jacob'. He did not say that he *was* their God. God creates us to live for ever.

Sunday 33(C)

Old Testament thought:
For you who fear my name, the sun of righteousness will
shine out with healing in his wings.   (Malachi 3.20)

Vocal prayer:
Sing psalms to the Lord with the harp,
with the sound of music.
With trumpets and the sound of the horn
acclaim the King, the Lord.
Let the sea and all within it thunder;
the world, and all its peoples.
Let the rivers clap their hands;
the hills ring out their joy
at the presence of the Lord.
For the Lord comes, comes to rule the earth.
He will rule the world with justice
and the peoples with fairness.   (From Psalm 98)

Gospel: Luke 21.5–19

For the Jew of our Lord's time, the Jerusalem Temple symbolized the presence of God upon earth. To foretell the destruction of his Temple was tantamount to foretelling the destruction of the world. By speaking of the destruction of the Temple Jesus was announcing the end of the Old Testament dispensation, and proclaiming the beginning, through his death and resurrection, of the final stage of God's reign upon earth. He himself joined with the members of his Body would become the new and everlasting Temple of God among men.

Jesus knew, however, that not only Jews but the early Christians, too, would apply his words about the destruction of the Temple to the end of the world; and so he warned his hearers against false notions about the end of all things. St Mark tells us plainly that Jesus said that the time of the End is known to God the Father alone.

But Jesus did announce that the end-time had come. At his resurrection the world entered the final stage of its history, and the catastrophic events that will take place during this end-time are all signs that an end will come, although never indications of the exact date when it will come.

Most important of all is our Lord's admonition to his disciples to persevere throughout times of great trial in lives of justice, purity, and love, and to maintain firm faith in his coming again to ensure the victory of good over evil.

Sunday 34(C): The Feast of Christ the Universal King

Old Testament thought:
All the tribes of Israel came to David in Hebron. 'Look,'
they said, 'we are your own flesh and blood.'

(2 Samuel 5.1)

Vocal prayer:
The Lord is my shepherd;
there is nothing I shall want.
Fresh and green are the pastures
where he gives me repose.
Near restful waters he leads me,
to revive my drooping spirit.
He guides me along the right path;
he is true to his name.

You have prepared a banquet for me
in the presence of my foes.
My head you have anointed with oil;
my cup is overflowing.

Surely goodness and kindness shall follow me
all the days of my life.
In the Lord's own house shall I dwell
for ever and ever.   (From Psalm 23)

Gospel: Luke 23.35–43

The Lord God will give him the throne of his ancestor
  David;
he will rule over the House of Jacob for ever
and his reign will have no end (Luke 1.33).

The cross makes these words of the angel Gabriel look
like a wicked lie. So thought the leaders of the people,
who jeered at him, so thought the soldiers, who mocked
him – 'If you are the King of the Jews, save yourself'. But
one of the criminals crucified beside Jesus thought otherwise. He pleaded humbly, using words that were a tradi-
tional supplication, 'Jesus remember me.' This man, by
the grace of God, discerned the true nature of kingship
and of power. He knew that the man dying beside him on
the cross, with no bitterness towards his tormentors, was
innocent, and he recognized the infinite power possessed
by this man, whose heart and will were perfectly at one
with the heart and will of God the Father whom he
trusted completely. This man, Jesus, had the power to
draw him and instil into him peace in the presence of
God. In his suffering and dying – the final proof of his
being true man – Jesus exerted the might of divine
majesty that was able to redeem mankind.

Royal glory was conferred upon Jesus not in spite of the
cross but because of the cross, for the cross was his opportunity to offer our human nature in total obedience and
faith to God the Father, thus reconciling us to the Father
and also to one another. The only effective power that the
Church or the individual Christian may ever exercise is
the power that Jesus displayed on the cross.

That which the prophet-king of old
Hath in mysterious verse foretold,
Is now accomplished, whilst we see
God ruling nations from a tree.

(Venantius Fortunatus AD 530–609)